Watch What You Hear

Penelope's Dream of Twenty Geese

Edward Teach

Cover painting by Jean-Léon Gérôme, *Le Rêve de l'Autre*.

ISBN 978-1-7344608-0-3
edwardteachmd@gmail.com

Table of Contents

οὐ γάρ ἐστιν κρυπτὸν ἐὰν μὴ ἵνα φανερωθῇ, οὐδὲ ἐγένετο ἀπόκρυφον ἀλλ' ἵνα ἔλθῃ εἰς φανερόν.

εἴ τις ἔχει ὦτα ἀκούειν ἀκουέτω. Καὶ ἔλεγεν αὐτοῖς· βλέπετε τί ἀκούετε.

For nothing is hidden if not to be made illuminated, nor became it hidden except to come to light. He who has ears to hear let him hear. Then he said to them: Watch what you hear.

--Mark 4:11

Introduction

It is likely unsurprising to classicists, or anyone, that psychoanalysis has failed to offer useful insights into Penelope's famous dream of twenty geese from Homer's Odyssey. But the deployment of psychoanalytic theory against literary mysteries is an established practice not merely for text elucidation but for the greater purpose of exploring human nature. As the Odyssey is already one of the oldest and most reliable texts on the human condition, it is thus remarkable how little psychoanalysis has been able to make of it.

Many investigators seem to equate psychodynamic theory with "repressed sexuality", gleefully declaring they have discovered Penelope's "secret" sexual desire, namely lust for one or all of the suitors. This banality hardly requires Freud's abstruse alchemy and has occurred to most adolescents living before television.

A critique of these and the many other unremarkable analyses is beyond the scope of this text, nor indeed generally useful. However, they share a single characteristic that is at the center of their failures: they are not interpreting the dream, they are interpreting the *plot* of the dream. Despite Freud's explicit instructions and warnings, these investigators have utterly ignored the mechanism of dream distortion. They assume the dream's symbolism is a pre-verbal, pictorial device driving to *convey* information, instead of the consequence of the dream's attempt to *hide* information. They take as axiomatic the converse of the analytic axiom: they assume the dream wants to be revealed. It does not[1]. Not coincidentally, the most overlooked of all of the mechanisms of dream *distortion* is the most important one, and also the only one that we have direct access to: the telling of the dream: by Penelope, to the beggar, in Greek, in poetic form[2].

---

1 Ironically, while conceding that the dream has a meaning beneath the chaos, what is overlooked is that the dream also has a purpose of which that chaos is a part. Freud based his model of the unconscious on the then trendy analogue of steam powered machines, while it is fashionable today to consider the brain as "digital processor" or "neural network"; which is the "best" analogy is pointlessly arguable, what is important is what is required by all of them: the unconscious may be complicated but it is rigorously logical. It is the conscious mind that deliberately subverts purpose by inventing meaning.

2 Freud takes this analogy even more literally than I do here:

> ...concrete terms, owing to their evolution, are *richer* than abstract terms. It may be imagined that a good part of the intermediate work in dream-formation, which seeks to reduce the separate dream thoughts to the tersest and most unified expression in the dream... is effected by fitting paraphrases of the various thoughts. The one thought whose mode of expression has perhaps been determined... exert[s] a distributive and selective influence on the expressions available for

Whether or not psychoanalysis is a reliable technique yielding valid results is not for me here to decide. But it deserves to be tried once.

To interpret Penelope's dream, a new approach is needed, which is the old approach: listen to the words[3].

---

the others... just as it would in the creative activity of a poet. When a poem is to be written in rhymed couplets, the second rhyming line is bound by two conditions: it must express the meaning allotted to it, and its expression must...rhyme. The best poems are, of course, those in which one does not detect the effort to find a rhyme... (Emphasis mine.) (SE, 6C.)

3 Its importance in modern daily speech negligible; in dream analysis axiomatic; but in Ancient Greek prosody almost obligatory. Rather than the language being forced into an artificial poetic meter, the language naturally fit the meter.

Even more pronounced in the ancient tradition is the use of multiple words with similar word stems to convey multiple meanings, as in Penelope's explanation of where dreams come from. After Odysseus gives his interpretation, Penelope responds that there are two kinds of dreams; some come from the gate of "horn" that are prophetic, and the others, which come through the gate of "ivory", which "deceive, bring no fulfillment". Murray (1919) remarked that something has been lost in (English) translation, but perhaps even more than he detected, because the original reads (19.565)

τῶν οἳ μέν κ᾽ ἔλθωσι διὰ πριστοῦ **ἐλέφ**αντος, οἵ ῥ᾽ **ἐλεφ**αίρονται ἔπε᾽ ἀκράαντα φέροντες

3

ἐλέφαντος, genitive of ἐλέφᾶς, both "ivory" and "elephant"; and ἐλεφαίρονται, which is translated "deceive" but connotes being denied proper fulfillment. Note the alternate gate of horn (κεράων), from which fulfilled (κραίνουσι) images pass (the opposite of ἀκράαντα). But a further important association is between the suffixes: ἐλε**φαίρονται** and **φέροντες**; the dreams don't deceive *by* bringing unfulfilled words, they *show* something as fulfilled that in real life is not. The dream is the manifestation of the fulfillment of a wish.

Flectere si nequeo superos, Acheronta movebo.

--Virgil

I am accustoming myself to regarding every sexual act as a process in which four people are involved. We shall have more to say about this.

--Freud

PRE-TEST:

1. What are the first words spoken *out loud* by a character in the Odyssey?

2. Why?

Nihil Obstat: The Interpretation Of The Dream

In Book 19, Odysseus has returned home disguised as a beggar, and Penelope tells the beggar a dream she had. I here use the Fagles translation (19.535) for reasons which will soon become apparent:

> But please, read this dream for me, won't you? Listen closely. I keep twenty geese in the house, from the water trough they come and peck their wheat — I love to watch them all. But down from a mountain swooped this great hook-beaked eagle, yes, and he snapped their necks and killed them one and all, and they lay in heaps throughout the halls while he, back to the clear blue sky he soared at once.

> But I wept and wailed — only a dream, of course – and our well-groomed ladies came and clustered round me, sobbing, stricken: the eagle killed my geese.

> But down he swooped again and settling onto a jutting rafter called out in a human voice that dried my tears, 'Courage, daughter of famous

King Icarius! This is no dream but a happy waking vision, real as day, that will come true for you. The geese were your suitors — I was once the eagle but now I am your husband, back again at last, about to launch a terrible fate against them all!'

So he vowed, and the soothing sleep released me. I peered around and saw my geese in the house, pecking at their wheat, at the same trough where they always took their meal.

Penelope asks the beggar (Odysseus) what he thinks this means. The beggar says the dream "can only mean one thing", and restates the eagle's interpretation: the wish/prophecy is that Odysseus will return and kill the suitors. The interpretation is fairly obvious; and it seems to reflect the deepest wishes of a faithful wife. The "twenty" is a minor difficulty given that there are 108 suitors but it could simply stand for an ambiguously large amount, the way Americans might hyperbolize using "a million" and 5th century Athenians used "300"[4]. Or it could be the result of

---

4 e.g. Thucydides, 5.84, within a single paragraph counts "300 Spartan suspects seized" by Athenians who then march on Melos with "300 archers." The number 300 appears over 60 times, counting years, men, the dead, horses, ships; but it is notably absent as a tally for what would require greater precision, e.g. talents, about which we hear 1/60, 1, 8, 9, 25, 30, 32, 33, 60, 90, 120, 200, 400, 460, 500, 800, 1000, 2000, 100000. "300 talents" does appear once (6.93), but in proximity to another number with two digit signifiant figure precision (300 talents, 250 horseless

condensation, multiple "twenties" manifested in one gaggle: the twenty years she's waited for her husband; the amount of time Odysseus had asked her to wait before re-marrying; Telemachus's age; the twenty ships Telemachus took to find news of Odysseus; the twenty men Antinous set in ambush for his return[5].

But these extra associations are merely supplemental and do not much affect the meaning. The main interpretation in the text and among readers remains the one given by the eagle in the dream.

It is wrong.

---

horsemen, 30 archers) suggesting that (unlike 5.84's suspects and archers) the 300 is here accurate to the tens place. Odysseus tells Athena with her by his side he would even fight 300 men (13.384). Interestingly, two sources cite the number of Penelope's suitors as 300 (Bassett, 1918) which suggests the increase is parabolic, or hyperbolic.

5 One might think "twelve" geese would at least have better fit the narrative and still preserve the meter, e.g "χῆνές μοι κατὰ οἶκον ἐείκοσι" could have been "χῆνές μοι κατὰ δόμον δυώδεκα", associating to the 12 ships of Odysseus, the 12 axes the eagle would "chew" through, the 12 princes of Ithaca, or the 12 shameful women Odysseus later hangs.

The Form Of Distortion In Dreams

The assertion that it is wrong is meant formally: the interpretation is *invalid*. The problem with the eagle's interpretation of the dream is that it isn't an interpretation; it is literally part of the manifest dream itself, and thus a distortion. Worse (e.g. more suggestive of a defensive distortion), it is *appended* to the dream by the dream as if to make sense of the dream; in fact, the interpretation is the second defense of this same "appended" form, the first is the *literal* addition of her crying, also occurring in the dream.

The dream occurs in distinct episodes, or acts. *First*, the eagle kills the geese and flies away. *Then* she cries and wails "though in a dream", and the women gather to comfort her. And *then* the eagle returns with the interpretation. But the eagle's interpretation, formally, is no different from the eagle itself; one would not presume that the eagle represents an actual eagle; neither is the interpretation the actual interpretation. The eagle's interpretation cannot be correct because the dream gave it. It is a defense.

The more fruitful approach would start from what can be observed-- the distortions-- and not the possible meanings. For example, if a person has an overtly sexual dream, the correct question to ask would be *why sexual*? What wish was so deeply repressed that it was safer to manifest it as sexual?[6] Here, one should ask not what do the geese represent, but why are they *geese*? Why not penguins? Some link between the manifest content (geese) and the latent content needs to be found; it could be a word, a recollection, a feeling, some quality; the link could even be unintelligible, as long as the dreamer is the one who makes the uncensored link ("I don't know why, but for some reason, goose makes me think of

---

6 Freud recounts a dream told to him by an (adult) woman (SE IV):

> She puts a candle in a candlestick, but the candle is broken, so that it does not stand up. The girls at school say she is clumsy; but she replies it is not her fault. An obvious symbolism has here been employed.

To be blunt: she may be clumsy, but her husband broke his own candle. But why would this "young woman, carefully brought up, and a stranger to all obscenity" choose such an obvious symbolism? What was its obviousness a defense against? To answer this, one begins with the distortions that seem irrelevant, as they will be least defended: why is she at school? In the course of the free association, she mentions that while paddling in a canoe on the Rhine, a boat passed her which contained some students who were singing:

> 'When the Queen of Sweden, behind closed shutters, with the candles of Apollo...' She does not hear or else understand the last word. Her husband was asked to give her the required explanation...

Only the free association reveals that the obvious interpretation of male impotence was a cover for the more inappropriate (to her) desire concerning masturbation.

14

X.") One cannot be satisfied with the obvious guesses[7], especially when the guess would have been obvious to the dreamer.

Add-ons in dreams are post-hoc distortions, trying to further hide the wish that might have been insufficiently hidden by the first round of dream distortions. But such

---

7 A similar mistake explains the misinterpretation that Penelope wishes the suitors to die so she could remain with the well groomed Achaean women, who attend to her *in the dream* during her grief *in the dream*. If one were looking for a latent sexual wish, 108 misogynists and a lifetime of enforced heterosexuality might plausibly suggest this unacceptable alternative would be obvious. But as obvious, one must ask: why are the women described *out loud* by awake Penelope as "well groomed"?

The word describing the "well groomed" Achaean women is ἐϋπλοκαμῖδες, better translated "well coiffed" or "braided" to capture the connotation of hair. Also prevalent is ἠύκομος (εὔκομος). Though Helen is famously blonde, her hair is described καλλικόμοιο, "beautifully haired," in keeping with her various other features which are beautiful (e.g. καλλιπάρηος, beautiful cheeked); while "blond(e)" (ξανθὸς) is not used for her but is nearly an honorific for Menelaus ("ξανθὸς Μενέλαος"). The word ἐϋπλόκαμος is used multiple times in the Odyssey, almost always for the supernatural (Calypso, Demeter, Dawn, Athena, Artemis and Circe; the nymphs (12.130 (but see also 12.375 "long robed"))) and the Phaeacian maidens (who are οἳ ἀγχίθεοι γεγάασιν, near kin of the gods (5.35)), possibly suggesting there is something remarkable or elevated about Penelope's attendants.

The link to Demeter is has a mythic parallel, sorrow for one that is in hell (which for Odysseus is metaphorically, yet also literally, accurate.) There was a well known cult of Demeter (surname Ἀχαιά or Ἀχαία) in Boeotia (Herod v. 61, Plut Is et Osiris p. 378 D.), suggesting a link to the Achaeans. Is it merely a coincidence that "Achaean" is similar to "axos" which means "mental anguish"? As Demeter was hardly the main god of the Achaeans, there's no reason she of all would earn that surname. Furthermore, the word Ἀχαία isn't correct as the description of a people

15

defenses are improvised and not very precise-- blunt and hasty instruments such as denial, reversal, or even forgetting[8], which hide the meaning but often unintentionally highlight that something was hidden. Like an imbalance in a painting that reflexively suggests something has been cut out, or the smell of bleach at what suddenly feels like a crime scene, the add-ons inadvertently, but inevitably, suggest the cover-up of a wish.

An immediate example of this type of distortion is one of "plot holes" which modern interpretations of the geese by

_____

(possibly Ἀχαιά, but almost always plural Ἀχαιοί); indeed, it was translated by some lexicographers as "the sorrowing one". In a Thespian inscription it is Ἀχέα, and may have been substituted with the homophone Ἀχαία, both explaining the odd placement of the accent and implicitly or explicitly retains (creates?) the analogy to grief. In this way, the fair haired Achaeans who gather to grieve with Penelope are the over-representation of anguish for the loss of something beloved.

But the unique binomial expression "well-coiffed Achaeans" (ἐυπλοκαμῖδες Ἀχαιαί) describing Penelope's attendants appears in only one other place: (2.110), Antinous compares Penelope's wiles to those of the ἐυπλοκαμῖδες Ἀχαιαί of old: Tyro, Alcmene, and Mycene. Thus, the dream makes a logically transitive connection between the dream attendants and the Achaeans women which Antinous had connected to Penelope. But their wiles have an ironic quality: Tyro and Alcmene both were seduced by gods pretending to be the men they loved; and whose children lost their birthrights. Hera maneuvered to prevent Alcmene's child from becoming ruler of the land; Tyro abandoned her twins on the mountain; Mycene's child was a monster which Hera deployed as a guard dog.

8 A key defense in the stories of the ancient world: forgetting everything, but knowing that something was forgotten. This should be noted wherever it occurs, and will be important later.

16

necessity cannot detect: if the dream geese are suitors, it is notably peculiar that she enjoyed watching them coming out of the water and eating-- *but why didn't the eagle's interpretation address this?* The reason that the eagle did not address that is because watching them wasn't *in* the dream. This is lost in English, where implied verbs are almost always expressed explicitly, e.g.

> I keep twenty geese in the house, from the water trough they come and peck their wheat.

The above sentence contains three active verbs (keep, come, peck). But the same in Greek:

> χῆνές μοι κατὰ οἶκον ἐείκοσι πυρὸν ἔδουσιν ἐξ ὕδατος

> twenty geese of mine of the house out of the water eating grain

has only has one active verb, ἔδουσιν, eat, in the present tense. She is telling the beggar *about* her geese, how it warms her heart looking at them (καί τέ σφιν ἰαίνομαι (present) εἰσορόωσα (participle)); while what she dreamt-- i.e. the movie events *of* the dream-- is described in the past tense (aorist). The eagle knows none of this; it does not know where they came from, or that she enjoyed watching them, or what they represented to her-- or even how many there were, and NB the number 20 does not repeat again-- these things are only part of Penelope's *telling* of the dream to the beggar. And it is in the telling of the dream that we will find the way to the correct interpretation.

The eagle's interpretation is representational, as if the dream were a pictogram like Egyptian hieroglyphics, it decrypts the images "geese" and "eagle" to suitors and Odysseus. But this isn't how one reads hieroglyphics, and fails for dream interpretation as well-- unless its purpose is a defense, a lie. Decrypting the images cannot explain why the geese are suitors, why they had pleased her, or why she would be sad about their deaths. *Nor can it explain why the eagle leaves afterwards.* In fact, the interpretation highlights these incongruities; this is the smell of bleach loudly pointing to something missing, it is the signal, "the return", of the repressed. The eagle's second appearance and interpretation are a separate dream-act, and are the manifestation of the fulfillment of separate wish. Because the wish declared is so obvious (Odysseus to return, suitors to die), and because it is appended, this strongly suggests that the wish is not hers, but someone else's: it is a wish she is *supposed* to have. It is Odysseus's wish.

In simple summary: the first part of the dream (the geese are killed) represents some latent desire of hers *which is unacceptable*; the second part (the eagle's return and interpretation) is the desire's further distortion into a more acceptable manifestation-- the acceptable desire of her husband, Odysseus's obvious desire to kill suitors. This succeeds in hiding Penelope's latent wish underneath a "superego appropriate" wish (in which the superego is Odysseus). But her latent wish (dream's first part) still *happened*. The incompatibility between what the eagle says it means and what the dream showed happening is the

18

synthesis of a latent *wish fulfillment* being covered and defended against by someone else's wish, it is the same as saying "Of course, you can see I've only ever wanted what you wanted! (But I still briefly got what I wanted)."

In the first part of the dream she was shown her wish fulfillment (distorted); in the second part, it was replaced with someone else's wish; the net result is that she has been deprived of her wish by this superego figure. In the dream, *but especially in reality*, she will wish that that figure be made to pay. Which is why the dream has a third part, or act.

In her description of the dream, Penelope tells the beggar that, after the eagle returns and declares that he is her husband the geese are suitors, she wakes up and sees that the geese are back. If the geese are *within the dream* now established to be the suitors, if the eagle wishes them dead, why would she say out loud that she saw them immediately up awakening? Why bring them back, behind his back? But this third part stands as an addendum to the addendum: if I must forced to accept the desire of the other-- if I must be deprived of my desire in whole or in part, then I can at least wish that the other is, after all, deprived of his.

Regardless of what the geese "symbolize", *this* is why she says they are there. It has nothing to do with her desire for the suitors to return, but is a strictly formal maneuver when she is deprived of her unconscious wish by someone else's desire which she is obligated to want. It deprives the other of their satisfaction, whatever it is. That the dream is not simply about her desire (i.e. the desire of an independent

19

adult who has the power to wish, *fantasize* for whatever they want, even if they know they shouldn't), but also structured like an Oedipal conflict between desires ("mine vs the Father's[9]") indicates a regression, and relates to the form of the third defense, which is the last distortion that occurs in the dream, and thus most primitive she employs: she closes the dream by going back at the beginning of the dream. It is

---

9 Oedipal refers to paternal (or in today's imprecise parlance 'patriarchal') authority, and the Homeric culture expected this authority to be cleanly transferred from her father to husband. But the unconscious cannot be traded for a dowry. A blatant manifestation of a superego (=husband) inappropriate wish should not have been possible; Penelope should have dreamt only the second part (the eagle's interpretation), or at best some complicated expression of her wish *within* his wish. That she was able to have the other two parts of the dream suggests that the husband's authority is not complete, and NB the eagle-- calling himself not "Odysseus" but "your husband"-- calls her neither by her name nor "my wife" but as "daughter of Icarius". She is still her father's daughter. More will be said concerning the phrase "daughter of X".

undoing.[10] [11]

The first part was the manifestation of the fulfillment of a wish. The second part was an attempt at distorting what was too much in conflict with desires she was supposed to have, by having them replaced by the "appropriate" desire of her husband. She then subverted his wishes in the third part. The result is that her desire remains intact, covered by a false wish, and hopefully beyond the reach of interpretation.

---

10 Undoing, in the conventional understanding, is a psychological defense in which a new behavior seeks to obliterate, undo, the consequences of an action: an abusive husband who then brings his wife flowers is not just making it up to her, but changing in his own mind that the facts of what happened define him. However, in order to properly interpret the dream psychoanalytically, we must use a more precise definition: undoing seeks to change not just the interpretation of the facts, but the past action *itself*. Here, the undoing would change for the husband the past reality; giving flowers makes it true that he did not, could not have, hit his wife. A slap perhaps, or she fell into his elbow, but he did not hit her. (It does not matter what her recollection or the video indicates.) In Penelope's dream, she not only undoes the meaning of the dream as given by the eagle, she makes it true that what the eagle did in fact did not happen. This distinction will become important in the discussion of the shroud.

11 Another, less common but more interesting maneuver is to dream she falls asleep and then has a within the dream. This is far from a complex unconscious maneuver, it is simply a primitive *denial*: I wish the thing in the inner vision, which is real, was just a dream (Freud VI C).

Imprimatur: When the Censor Is Not Enough

Yet while the dream does not want to be interpreted, she begs the beggar for an interpretation. Why not ignore the dream, or even forget it all together? Because the unconscious wish is becoming too knowable. She suspects she has the inappropriate wish, as evidenced by the Herculean efforts at distorting it within the dream. Here becomes crucial another unconscious defense against dream interpretation: *the choice of interpreter*. No matter what they say, dreamers *do not want to know* the meaning of the dream-- otherwise it would not have been distorted. So she chooses an interpreter who *appears to be* one who would know the meaning, but hopes he would not know it, or could be fooled; his utility is in that he has the power to *authorize* an acceptable interpretation[12].

---

12 The desire for the beggar to have the role of the omnipotent (not omniscient) interpreter is signaled by Penelope's own demand (19.535):

ἀλλ᾽ ἄγε μοι τὸν ὄνειρον **ὑπόκριναι** καὶ *ἄκουσον*

But come now, **hear** this dream of mine, and **interpret** it for me.

NB the reversal in the English translation. The Greek says "interpret"

He appears omniscient, but is in fact only omnipotent. And he can be fooled. This is why a psychoanalyst would (should) never interpret a patient's dream for the patient; he can note it to himself, but his role is only to facilitate free association. Even a correct interpretation can still be misheard or misused by the patient in unpredictable ways; to authorize any interpretation to the patient is to be complicit in the cover-up[13].

---

then "hear". Did the English serve the text by clarifying the meaning, or Penelope's unconscious by further distorting the meaning? The reversal is dismissed as rhetorical prothysteron, in which the more important word is placed (atemporally) before the first, except Penelope does not previously use this device in her own speech. Taken literally, however, it suggests that the interpretation is to occur before the hearing-- i.e. she wants him to give the interpretation he (and she) already has, that she knows he wants to give even without hearing it.

Reinforcing this, a second complication is that both verbs are aorist imperative. Part of the trickiness is the aspect; hardly a command in the past tense, but rather implies an action that is to be done in its entirety: "hear immediately", "interpret immediately". This has a special valence when the verb can take a long time or a short time: "find it" (present imperative: start the process of finding, that may take you some time) and "find it" (aorist imperative: find it right now!)

Here, the aorist imperative wants the job done. The complication, however, is that "interpret" is middle voice while "hear" is in the active. A roundabout way to capture the meaning might be: "hear all of it completely" but "interpret all of it [for] yourself completely"-- interpret it all as you *want* it to mean. Taken together, what Penelope is requesting is what bad dream interpreters do all the time: while they hear the dream told to them, they fit the dream into the interpretation they already "know"/want it to have.

13 All of this applies equally to psychoanalysis in general. The patient's bet is that the analyst is supposed to know such things (everyone else

23

So like a murderer calling the police to investigate the crime scene she's already sterilized with bleach, she goes to the beggar for his help, not because he will know the meaning, but because she knows he *cannot* know the meaning, he doesn't even know what bleach is; yet has the power to declare the dream to mean something else. He appears omniscient[14] but can be fooled; he is an omnipotent

---

would agree he would know) but hopes realistically he could not know, yet has the power to authorize the interpretation. But neither would (should) the analyst *say* he doesn't know the interpretation, as his role as "the one who knows" is necessary to the analytic process. Hence the stereotypical *frustrating* exchanges such as this one: "Doctor, do you think it means X?" – Why don't you tell me why you think it means that? "Agh! Why can't you be straight with me?" --Is my being straight something you need me to be? Etc. The goal in analysis is not to give the patient knowledge about himself, but to facilitate the taking of power.

14 Knowledge and action are always in inverse proportion (consider the Delphic Oracle); who has knowledge and who can act are distinct, and these roles are dyadic, they depend on the specific relationship between them. e.g. Antinous (NB: "against knowledge", compare Alcinous (Ἀλκίνοος, "elk (-strong) knowledge"); and as a free association, recall that the other Alcinous who commented on the Cratylus: "A name is the instrument that corresponds to a thing, not attached randomly, but appropriate to its nature… it is a tool which teaches and distinguishes") on why they should kill Telemachus:

> [Telemachus] is *sophisticated* in **counsel** and intelligence

> αὐτὸς μὲν γὰρ ἐπιστήμων **βουλῇ** τε νόῳ τε

Penelope rebukes him (16.420):

> men say that in Ithaca you are the **best** ever in **counsel** and **speech**. But you are not such man.

24

entity who can be fooled into authorizing a different meaning.

To be clear: the different meaning authorized by the interpreter does not need to be completely wrong. What is required is merely that the interpretation does not identify the unacceptable wish.

Of course "fooled" is not a conscious deception, but an

ὁμήλικας ἔμμεν **ἄριστον βουλῇ** καὶ **μύθοισι**

But earlier we had a basis for how to use these comparisons: Athena says to the disguised Odysseus (13.295)

> But come, let us no longer say these things when both of us know *cunning* ways,
>
> since you among all mortals are by far the **best** in **counsel** and **speech**,
>
> and I among gods am famed for my intelligence and *craft*
>
> ἀλλ᾽ ἄγε, μηκέτι ταῦτα λεγώμεθα, εἰδότες ἄμφω **κέρδε᾽**,
>
> ἐπεὶ σὺ μέν **ἐσσι** βροτῶν ὄχ᾽ **ἄριστος** ἁπάντων **βουλῇ καὶ μύθοισιν**,
>
> ἐγὼ δ᾽ ἐν πᾶσι θεοῖσι μήτι τε κλέομαι καὶ **κέρδεσιν**.

While Antinous (2.115) claimed

> Athena has endowed [Penelope] above other women with knowledge of fair handiwork and an understanding heart, and *wiles*

25

unconscious quid pro quo between the dreamer and the interpreter, who is made to feel appreciated, wise, insightful-- omniscient. *The form of having a dream interpreted symbolically by a seemingly omniscient, but actually only omnipotent person who can be fooled--* fooled by giving him what *he* wants, in exchange for a false interpretation-- that pattern-- is itself the mark of repression. One of the ways analysts guard against becoming such a fooled omnipotent entity is having a higher supervisor review the case. Of course, it is not difficult to imagine that the initial analyst could unconsciously set up the supervisor to be another omnipotent entity, and fool him into confirming his interpretation; now, for the patient, the false interpretation has been authorized by two omnipotent entities and approaches dogma.

δῶκεν Ἀθήνη ἔργα τ᾽ ἐπίστασθαι περικαλλέα καὶ
φρένας ἐσθλὰς **κέρδεά** θ᾽

From this, in counsel and speech, Antinous is no Odysseus. Penelope is like Athena and Odysseus in her (cunning) crafts. Telemachus is sophisticated in counsel and intelligence-- but not superlative. Antinous has know knowledge (but he acts repeatedly.) Athena is said to have English "intelligence", but the word μῆτι is better translated as "plannings"; and craft more than all. She is in theory the goddess of wisdom, but in the Odyssey she is the goddess of action, cunning, and plannings. (And note Zeus's specific criticism of her at the end, 24.475, when the suitors' kin unite to attack: "you're asking me now what I have planned? All of this is your doing!" To stop the final slaughter, he throws down a thunderbolt-- at *her*.) However, the only one who has the power of speech-- the ability to declare things true-- and lacks knowledge-- is Odysseus.

26

This is precisely what Homer[15] has done with us: the supervising audience of readers has been lead to believe it is omniscient so that it can be fooled into authorizing as true the eagle's interpretation which is false.

---

15 Though analysis is beyond the scope of this paper, "Homer" here refers not to a single individual (even if, indeed, a single individual composed the poem initially) but the entire ecclesiastical tradition of Homeric poets, who unconsciously worked to make the poem free of dogmatic errors.

Abduction: If It Looks Like A Duck

This may seem preposterous, until one recalls that the readers of the Odyssey already know what the goose and eagle represent even before the eagle comes back to explain it, because that dream already happened. Earlier (15.160) Telemachus is leaving the house of Menelaus, and as everyone gathers around his chariot to say good-bye, they look up and see an eagle snatching a goose. What could this omen[16] mean? Helen interprets it: it is an omen for Telemachus. Just as the eagle comes from the crags and snatches the goose, so Odysseus will come home and take revenge on the suitors. Telemachus welcomes the interpretation. Now the reader of the Odyssey has been told what "goose" and "eagle" symbolize, so the dream-eagle's interpretation and the beggar's confirmation are only further affirmation of what the audience already knows.

Except Helen's interpretation is not just wrong, it is not even internally consistent. Several men have just witnessed the omen. Orienting ourselves to the gender norms of the time, why is Helen allowed to give an interpretation? According to Telemachus (1.355 *and* 23.350), women belong at the loom, speech (μῦθος) (and NB the bow) is for men,

---

16 That it is an omen to be interpreted is signaled by the eagle coming in from the right and flying away to the right; see also 15.545.

especially for Telemachus because he has the power in his house (μῦθος δ᾿ ἄνδρεσσι μελήσει πᾶσι, μάλιστα δ᾿ ἐμοί: τοῦ γὰρ κράτος).   Whose house are they in now, under this logic what man has the power to speak? But Helen has to speak up and usurp the power, because it isn't Telemachus's omen, it's Menelaus's.

The problem she faces is these men are looking for omens, they are looking to apply meaning; their dinner discussion had been about the duplicitous Clytemnestra (NB: perhaps Helen's fraternal or identical twin sister, or her-- nemesis[17]); childless Menelaus had wistfully admired Nestor's excellent children. And Helen has just told a dinner tale that is almost reckless in its boldness, tauntingly provocative: she begins by innocently explaining how Odysseus had snuck into Troy dressed as a slave, but she recognized him; and then proceeds to elaborate, *out loud*, that she then bathed him-- not had him bathed, but gave him a bath-- and swore not to tell the Trojans.[18]   Greek wine was diluted 1:3, making it difficult to quantify how much a Spartan warlord would need to drink to be able to listen to his

---

17 Worth remembering here is the conception of Helen according to Euripides: Zeus was a swan, chased by an eagle into the arms of Leda (human); they conceived Helen. This version was not likely known to Homer. However, the 7th century *Cypria* described a version more likely known to Homer, consistent with the Odyssey and at least anatomically plausible: Nemesis turned herself into a goose to escape Zeus, who then changed into a goose to rape her.

18 To be clear: it is customary to bathe guests, even strangers, as a symbol of hospitality. It is not at all customary for the wife to do the bathing; and note that Penelope did not bathe her visitor-- or the other 108.

wife tell this tale without reaching for a spear, or another drink, which is why Helen took no chances and drugged it. Nevertheless, Menelaus is still able to describe how while the Achaeans were hiding inside the Trojan horse, she had tried to tempt them out by pretending to be their wives[19]. Now an eagle snatches a goose right in from of them, and it requires only minimal creativity, lingering resentment or functioning hepatocytes for any of them to remember that the last time an eagle took a goose from Menelaus's house, the goose didn't put up a fight but everyone else had to. They said nothing, however, Egyptian drugs must have been very reliable. Even

---

19 It must be emphasized that almost the entire Homeric telling of the Trojan horse comes from this single passage. Of course the story was known from other sources, but not this exact scene sequence (it is not even clear that the Anticlus sentence was in the pre 6th century versions). Thus, this passage refers to nothing else but itself. If she had wanted to expose them, she could have simply said there were Achaeans in the horse. Not doing this makes sense if she wanted to avoid explaining to the Trojans how she knew this, because how she knew it was that she had just given Odysseus a bath, for which there is no explanation. It is preposterous that the Achaeans were fooled and believed their wives were right outside; and the passage does not really imply this. Everyone inside must have known it was Helen, *therefore* taunting them; and in this light, one can imagine the rage of Menelaus. Of course, Menelaus here says Odysseus had to hold back Anticlus, "who alone wanted to answer you" ἀμείψασθαι ἐπέεσσιν ἤθελεν, and this might be a bit of displacement; because rather than what the English implies-- that Anticlus was seduced by her voice-- we should take Menelaus's words literally: "wanted to answer you" here is the same expression used in 3.145 to describe Menelaus answering=screaming at Agamemnon (3.145) about whether to stay or go: χαλεποῖσιν ἀμειβομένω ἐπέεσσιν ἔστασαν, which Fagles diplomatically translates "wrangling", despite the surrounding words: "feuding", "wrath", "armour clashing", "ungodly uproar", and "seething".

30

so, what causes Helen to hastily declare this eagle is an omen for Telemachus is Peisistratus's asking *out loud* if this was not in fact an omen for Menelaus. But it's not enough to deny it is an omen or say it has no meaning-- that denial wouldn't *take*; she quickly assumes the role of prophetess-- she is many things in the text, but predictor of the future is not one of them-- and authorizes it to mean something else. To be clear: the authorized interpretation does not care if the interpretation is correct or incorrect, only that it does not identify the objectionable material.

One would be forgiven for not picking this up reading Fagles:

> At his last words, a bird flew past on the right, an eagle clutching a huge white goose in its talons, plucked from the household yards.
>
> [...]But long-robed Helen stepped in well before him: "Listen to me and I will be your prophet, sure as the gods have flashed it in my mind and it will come to pass, I know it will. Just as the eagle swooped down from the crags where it was born and bred, just as it snatched that goose fattened up for the kill inside the house, just so, after many trials and roving long and hard, Odysseus will descend on his house and take revenge..."

Greek, with my more literal translation:

31

ὣς ἄρα οἱ εἰπόντι ἐπέπτατο δεξιὸς ὄρνις

αἰετὸς ἀργὴν χῆνα φέρων ὀνύχεσσι πέλωρον,
ἥμερον ἐξ αὐλῆς

an eagle took [as if it was a prize] the radiant/idle goose in its talons [the goose that was] monstrous, tame, from the yard...

δ' Ἑλένη τανύπεπλος ὑποφθαμένη φάτο μῦθον:
κλῦτέ μευ: αὐτὰρ ἐγὼ μαντεύσομαι, ὡς ἐνὶ θυμῷ ἀθάνατοι βάλλουσι καὶ ὡς τελέεσθαι ὀΐω.

Flowing robed Helen hastily/in advance declared the word: "hear me, I will prophesy, as the immortals have put in my soul and it will in the end happen

ὡς ὅδε χῆν' ἥρπαξ' ἀτιταλλομένην ἐνὶ οἴκῳ

ἐλθὼν ἐξ ὄρεος, ὅθι οἱ γενεή τε τόκος τε, ὣς Ὀδυσεὺς

Just as this goose [the eagle] snatched, that was reared in the home,

[the eagle] that came from the mountains, from where are his family, and his birth; so

Odysseus..."

We might accept that Helen might want to avoid referring to certain facets of the omen; but it is interesting that Fagles's translation reinforces Helen's spoken misinterpretation by distorting the *narrative* description of the omen. Helen says the eagle is Odysseus, which is both geographically and genealogically incorrect, because she says that the eagle has its origins and family not in the house but in the ὄρεος-- *mountain*-- which is the exact same word (ὄρεος) Penelope says her dream eagle came from-- but which Fagles inexplicably though helpfully mystifies to "crags." The eagle isn't returning to its house, it is invading it, and it is worth noting that the suitors aren't from Ithaca at all, they are from the mountains of Kephallenia[20]. Meanwhile, the goose is explicitly of the house, hardly analogous to suitors occupying it. Helen's explanation is utterly backwards: the omen in fact shows an outsider invading the house and taking what is of it; not an insider returning to the house to expel what came from without.

The pitfalls of translating poetry are well known, words are obliged to carry multiple meanings, thus ignoring or changing a word can have the semantic consequences of

---

20 I am aware of the scholarship that attempts to place Penelope/Odysseus in Paliki, Kephallenia. This would not alter the argument here, as this hypothesis raises the ocean level and makes ancient Paliki an island, separate from Kephallenia; it is only today contiguous with Kephallonia because the sea has sufficiently receded. As a personal observation, the only modern Greeks who believe Odysseus is from Kephallenia are Kephallonians.

misplacing the decimal point and not knowing by how many places, which direction, or that it happened at all. This is doubly true for dreams and omens. The narrative describes the goose with three adjectives: ἀργὴν, πέλωρον and ἥμερον. Which of those words did Helen address? Even in the original Greek Helen only glancingly acknowledges ἥμερον, saying the goose was "ἀτιταλλομένην ἐνὶ οἴκῳ, reared in the house"; Fagles elaborates her words to "fattened for the kill inside the house", no doubt hoping to link it to the suitors feasting before their own slaughter. But Helen makes no Greek comment about what the goose looks like-- ἀργὴν and πέλωρον are ignored.

It is certainly possible that Helen did not perceive the goose as ἀργὴν, πέλωρον, or even ἥμερον. But Fagles did perceive them right there in the narration, yet he translated ἀργὴν as "white" and πέλωρον as "huge"; and ἥμερον is completely avoided, muted into a location ("plucked from the household yards"). But the Greek carries considerably different implications: ἀργὴν is not white (the hue) but radiant, iridescent (dictionary examples would include pearl or a peacock's tail[21]), and also "idle"-- not so much as in "bored" but as in "kept". This dovetails with the word Fagles avoided, ἥμερον: "tame"; and it is juxtaposed-- literally right next to-- πέλωρον: not "huge" referring to size, but "monstrous"; it is a word Homer uses as an adjective for only

_____

21 As further evidence for the work of condensation: Ἀργὴν is derived from ἀργός, which is also the name of Hera's many eyed giant sent to "guard" her husband's temptress (and also the name of Odysseus's loyal (black) dog). When Argos was killed by Hermes, Hera removed his eyes and put them on the feathers of the peacock.

a few other nouns: the Gorgon's head (11.634), the wolves and lions bewitched by Circe (10.219), the Cyclops (9.258).[22] Helen as goose is a remarkable member of this club, not just the only human but also the only instance in the book of πέλωρος in the feminine (Gorgon's *head* is masculine)[23]; and the only instance of ἥμερον at all. The narration sets up the goose to embody the complexity of Helen: radiant, kept, tamed, but also-- not huge in size-- but monstrous. Monstrous enough that Menelaus managed to remember through a drug induced fog what she did at the foot of the Trojan horse. Guilt or shame might explain why Helen would want to avoid these associations; it's possible only countertransference can explain why Fagles misses them[24].

---

22 When size is to be emphasized, the derivative used comes from πελώριος, e.g. Sisyphus's stone (11.594) and the waves that scattered the ships (3.290). The interesting exception to this is 10.169, πέλωρος stag-- but it is explicitly described in both its natural form (too big to carry this "huge beast" μέγα θηρίον) and distinctly its supernatural form ("feet of this monstrous creature" πόδας δεινοῖο πελώρου—NB the same phrase used for the Gorgon's head).

23 Goose (χῆνα) is feminine accusative, so of course πέλωρον is understood feminine; but this is the only feminine noun for which it is used. If "gigantic" was the desired meaning, it could have taken πελώρια (though admittedly this would have affected the meter). The unique choice of πέλωρον here must refer not to size but to its otherwise ubiquitous usage for supernaturally "monstrous" entities-- including goose sized ones like the Gorgon's head.

24 For whom is this description? As the omen is for Menelaus, the adjectives relate to his perception of his wife. Consider also "long robed Helen" or "Helen of the long robes" (Ἑλένη τανύπεπλος), which sounds like a fitting public honorific for Helen, except that it is used only for her one other time, 4.305, when she is in bed with him. It does find usage in (only) two other places: 1) for the nymph Lampetie-- but in her role as

Fagles is hardly alone in this; Murray (1919) translates the omen as "a great white goose, a tame fowl"; Fitzgerald only translates one adjective ("white") and the most recent translation by Wilson includes "tame" but unfortunately the goose is still "big" and "white." But Wilson changes Helen's description of the goose from "ἀτιταλλομένην ἐνὶ οἴκῳ-- reared in the yard" to "this tame goose". By duplicating in Helen's mouth the same English word used to describe the omen, she suppresses Helen's Greek admission of why it is tame: it isn't in someone's house, it is *someone's*.

The correct reading of eagle stealing the goose is an invader stealing a woman; not the respectable way, not by conquering the house like a proper warrior, but a grab and dash, a miscreant stealing a pie from the window sill and then feeling pretty good about his assertiveness; and it is an omen for Menelaus, signaled by Peisistratus's question. Helen reverses it to an omen for Telemachus about a husband heroically killing rivals nesting in his home. Everyone, but importantly Menelaus, accepts this. Menelaus accepts it because he does not want to know what he would know it means, and even if Peisistratus or Telemachus thought otherwise, they were not going to correct her. To be precise: they do not accept what she says as if she was omniscient-- she is not-- but accept that in this she has the power to declare things true. Confirming herself as an authority, she

shepherd and messenger, quickly telling Helios that the flock has been killed (12.375), not by Odysseus, but by his *men*; 2) for Ctimene, the sister of Odysseus, by the shepherd Eumaeus to indicate he was as loved as the noble daughter of the house.

36

announces that her knowledge isn't hers, but comes directly from the gods[25]. And Telemachus even reveals he does not think Helen herself is omniscient here-- she is not a prophetess-- but accepts her divine authority: "if only it were true! I'll pray to you as a goddess[26]!"[27]

Helen prepares the reader to accept the interpretation of

---

[25]NB parallel to Daniel's interpretation of Nebuchadnezzar's dream: Daniel interprets the dream not by any knowledge of his own, but directly under God's power. The question is not whether Daniel knows the interpretation, but whether Nebuchadnezzar will accept what Daniel declares it means. (He does-- and does not; c.f. *SP*.)

[26] Gods may appear omniscient, but except for Zeus they are merely omnipotent. Athena as Mentes says to Telemachus (1.230), "I'll make you a prophecy, one the immortal gods have planted in my mind— it will come true, I think, though I am hardly a seer or know the flights of birds…"

[27] There are three other bird vs. bird omens, which Telemachus witnesses himself; the key to their interpretation again lies in identifying whom the omen is *for*.

In 2.145, Antinous warns Telemachus to get his mother wed, but Telemachus refuses. He tells the suitors that if they think eating another man's livelihood without atonement is good, then go ahead and waste it, but he calls upon Zeus: without atonement, all of them should be destroyed within the house (δόμων, not οἶκον). Zeus "answers" with an omen: two eagles (from the mountains) swoop in, and with death in their eyes start clawing each other, then fly away to the right. The suitors wondered at it, and in their heart pondered its meaning; Halitherses offers the required interpretation:

> Hearken now to me, men of Ithaca, to the word that
> I shall say; and to the wooers especially do I declare
> and announce these things, since on them a great
> woe is rolling. For Odysseus shall not long be away

37

Penelope's dream-- and, if we can be permitted a parallel, in the same way Helen prepared Telemachus and Menelaus: by drugging them with deliciousness and then telling them what they want to hear. Both Penelope and Helen interpret the symbols in the exact same incorrect way, which could be suspicious; both women offer their interpretations unsolicited, which is the noxious smell of bleach that should be very

---

> from his friends, but even now, methinks, he is near,
> and is sowing death and fate for these men, one and
> all.

He's right, but wrong nevertheless; and it is worth highlighting that Halitherses is first introduced in 2.155 not as a prophet but as γέρων ἥρως, "old lord" (or old noble); and even his name (Ἁλιθέρσης) is derived not from ἀληθεύω "to speak the truth" but ἁλος "salt/ocean" and θάρσος "bravery". Power/authority, not knowledge, is emphasized in this "prophet"; and if one doubts this, Homer says it himself: ὄρνιθας ἐκέκαστο γνῶναι καὶ ἐναίσιμα μυθήσασθαι-- unsurpassed in a) knowledge of birds, and b) in speaking forebodings. Knowledge is not contained in the latter clause, and it isn't very complete in the former either. Zeus didn't send an eagle to claw *at* the suitors, he sent two eagles *to* the suitors which clawed each other. The entire basis for eagle=Odysseus equivalence requires different birds for the predator and prey, and here as early as Book 2 this is undermined. The correct interpretation is of suitors attacking suitors, the very outcome Antinous accused Penelope of fostering by shrewdly making promises to each as she delayed at the weaving. As will be explained, at this point the suitors have not yet become rivals of one another. That this would eventually be inevitable should have occurred to some suitors (and likely did), so their bafflement at the omen is a desire not to know; and Halitherses saves them from it by repackaging the omen for the purpose of confirming another prophecy he made earlier about Odysseus's return.

But one should observe that Halitherses doesn't give an interpretation of

38

suspicious. No one notices. Consequently, the audience is primed to believe that eagle stands for Odysseus and goose stands for suitor. That there are 20 geese in the dream and not 108 is thus to be explained away as approximation, referencing other twenties, or-- using the kill switch of dream interpretation-- simply declared irrelevant.

---

the omen; in fact, he makes absolutely no reference to it. He makes a prediction, the prediction is correct, but it has nothing at all to do with the omen as it *will be* interpreted. Eurymachus takes Halitherses's prediction and he himself applies it back to the omen, easily (and correctly) saying that Halitherses's words have nothing to do with what they just saw. But it is not enough to say that Halitherses's "interpretation" is wrong-- this leaves the omen open to further interpretation; he must deny that it is an omen at all. This is easy to do because he doesn't see Halitherses as a prophet-- he sees him as an old man, even if lord.

In (15.545), Telemachus is talking to Theoclymenus about Eurymachus possibly ending up marrying his mother, and wonders if Zeus's judgment on the suitors won't come first. Suddenly, a bird flies by (NB to the right) clutching another bird, defeathering it and dropping them in front of Telemachus. Theoclymenus declares it as a bird of omen (οἰωνὸς-- NB sharing etymology with οἰὸς, alone). Telemachus exclaims: "would that this word of thine be fulfilled!" But this omen is quite different from the others: first, despite Telemachus witnessing the two other omens that were not for him that involved eagles, the birds in *his* omen here are a hawk (κίρκος) and a dove (πέλειαν); but more importantly, the obvious interpretation *cannot* be a distortion, lie, or even mistake, because *no one actually gives it*. The reader is left to form his own interpretation. This is shown in the differences in nouns: the ἔπος, the "word [of thine]" that Telemachus wishes to be true is Theoclymenus's "word" (declaration) that it *is* an omen; when Homer describes that Helen hastily "spoke the word" (φάτο μῦθον), "word" there is the *interpretation*. Compare also 1.357, above, μῦθος δ᾽ ἄνδρεσσι, "words (discussions/interpretations) are for men". Even in 17.150, Theoclymenus tells Penelope about that same omen, he calls the hawk an οἰωνὸς, which Theoclymenus defined as a bird

But that's not why there are twenty geese in the dream, *because there aren't twenty geese in the dream*. "Twenty" isn't in the dream, it's in Penelope's telling of the dream; and it's not the *number* twenty but the *word* twenty. The geese are of the *house*, and the word twenty sounds like the word house, the word twenty tries to divert, shift, the attention from

---

of omen in 15.530. In general, the choice of birds relates not to any fixed symbolic referent (e.g. eagles stand for kings, or Odysseus) but is interpretable only in its *form* within a context-- exactly like a dream.

There is a final bird omen, useful in its contrast to cite here. After a long conversation ending with a prophecy of Odysseus's return, the very next sentence (20.240) cuts to the house where the suitors were "plotting the murder of Telemachus", and an eagle clutching a dove convinces Amphinomus to decide that their plot should be aborted-- they all agree, and have a party instead. Rutherford's commentary is typical (1992 p.224):

> The omen obviously foreshadows the hero's victory
> over the suitors, for the eagle as king of the birds,
> and representative of Odysseus, cf 19.538-50
> (Penelope's dream)...

Rutherford feels justified in deducing that the eagle implicitly prophesies Odysseus's return, likely because it comes on the wings of the previous scene in which Odysseus was explicitly prophesied to return; except that the explicit prophecy hardly counts as prophecy because a) it was made by Odysseus himself; b) he had *already* returned. And it requires considerable optimism to hope that the suitors would have thought the eagle was Odysseus because it would require that they see themselves as timid doves; and it requires us to overlook that Homer writes "*nevertheless* to them from the *left* came an eagle clutching a timid dove" αὐτὰρ ὁ τοῖσιν ἀριστερὸς ἤλυθεν ὄρνις, αἰετὸς ὑψιπέτης, ἔχε δὲ τρήρωνα πέλειαν. The eagle is they themselves. The omen does not *predict* that they will fail to kill Telemachus, it is *advising* them they shouldn't:

40

the word house by paraphrastic assonance[28], οἶκος (oy-kos, house) and ἐείκοσι (ee-i-kos-i, twenty). Penelope's description of "twenty" reaches back four words to modify geese but in a textbook example of metonymic slippage, the word twenty is literally placed next to the word house:

χῆνές μοι κατὰ οἶκον ἐείκοσι

geese (of mine) of the house twenty

The twenty *is* the house; the geese are the distortion, chosen because they are easily misinterpreted; what's being destroyed isn't the twenty geese in the house, but the twenty-house of the geese.

If one wanted to explain the equivalence "house is twenty", they might say something like "in this metaphor, the house, οἶκος, is analogous to twenty, ἐείκοσι"; or "the house manifests as, appears like, twenty." If one didn't want to explain it-- if one wanted to obfuscate the relation, shift the meaning-- one would remove the words "analogous to" or "appears like": οἶκος ἐείκοσι[29]. What makes this thought

---

"Friends, this plan of ours will not run to our liking, *even the slaying of Telemachus*..." (emphasis mine).

28 The relevance of paraphrastic assonances are one of the key insights of psychoanalysis: that the meanings of words may be entirely irrelevant or even distractions; they could be treated only as sounds (or even images), and can thus also carry across languages, e.g. Freud's link between a patient's use of the English phrase "it is *from* [one of Schiller's works]" to the German word *fromm,* pious; or "dysentery" for "hysteria" (6A2.)

29 Do these words rhyme? In modern Greek οἶκος and εἴκοσ(ι) and rhyme perfectly, the first syllables pronounced with a long "ee" (e.g.

process psychoanalytically interesting is that the Greek word for "appears like" and "analogous to", here removed, is yet another pseudo-homophone: eoik-o.   οἶκος ἔοικέι ἐείκοσι[30].

χῆνές μοι κατὰ οἶκον ἐείκοσι ἐξ ὕδατος, καί τέ σφιν ἰαίνομαι εἰσορόωσα

geese (of mine) of the house twenty...

ἐλθὼν δ᾽ ἐξ ὄρεος (mountain) μέγας αἰετὸς ἀγκυλοχείλης

"economy").   Without delving into the controversy about whether Erasmus was duped and patrimonial pride, or whether any of the non-barbarian tongues sounded similar (is it ee-conomy or uh-conomy, and is the standard rhotic King George III or a graduate of Eaton with his newly received pronunciation?-- and never mind Scots or Texans); even in the most Anglicized (Americanized?) rendering of Homeric Greek οἶκος merely adds an articulated prefix vowel to the long "ee"; they form not a digraph of a single sound but a diphthong of two sounds: /oy/ =oy-ee; and the disappearance of the "o" in the Modern Greek is likely a consequence of rapid and regular use of Greek emphasizing the second vowel of the diphthong (in contrast to English which typically emphasizes the first, consider "oil" where o>i.) It is worth recounting the famous homonym that caused Pericles's Athenians such consternation: whether the ancient prophecy had *out loud* said a Doric war shall come and bring *famine* (λιμός, lee-MOS) or *pestilence* (λοιμός, lee-MOS) (Thucydides, 2.54). They had no recourse to phonic analysis. The correct meaning was, of course, democratically decided.

30 Perhaps coincidentally, a similar simile built on (a different) periphrastic assonance can be created using the word twelve: δόμος δοκέι (μοι) δυώδεκα-- but this would lose the important distinction between δόμος and οἶκος.

πᾶσι κατ' **αὐχένας** ἦξε καὶ ἔκτανεν: οἱ δ'
ἐκέχυντο

all by **throat** broke and killed; *poured*

ἀθρόοι ἐν μεγάροις, ὁ δ' ἐς αἰθέρα δῖαν ἀέρθη.

In heaps in the hall, then into heaven divine
[the eagle] took off...

Similarly, "neck" (αὐχένας) associates to "geese"
(χῆνές)-- in fact, αὐχήν and χήν share etymology-- and also to
"piled in the hall" (ἐκέχυντο, from χέω) such that these are
not to be taken as distinct points of emphasis but as
distortions, smudges, residues, of the word which was
removed from the dream: Penelope. Which means goose.

That Penelope (Homer) is struggling with her
unconscious is justified by the text; she has two dreams to
interpret within only a few pages, and has already deployed
portmanteau (19.595) to invent another name for Troy,
"Cacoilium" (κακο (evil) + ἴλιον (Ilium) = "Κακοΐλιον"[31] [32]])
which is clever and considerably more intuitive than the
bafflingly obtuse rendering by Fagles, "Destroy", and the

---

31 Of course, this portmanteau word was made consciously and
deliberately, which means it isn't an unconscious portmanteau and thus
doesn't serve an unconscious purpose of condensing two ideas into a
single noun. It is more properly a compromise formation, a defensive
cover, between two ideas, something that is evil and something that comes
from Ilios.

32 How did Penelope pronounce Κακοΐλιον?

43

even worse anti-translation by Murray --"Evil Ilios"-- which is blamelessly precise as a transliteration but completely undoes the motivation for the compromise formation: that the actual city *must not be named* (οὐκ ὀνομαστήν).

In the ancient world words have power, and only a culture based in television would think a picture is worth a thousand of them. Penelope hid a whole household in a single conspicuous numeral, the naming of a number, and in both Helen's and Penelope's cases the necessary men blessed the necessary interpretation of eagle vs. goose = husband vs. suitor, because the interpretation aligned with *their men's* wish to hunt geese.

But the correct parallel to Helen's omen is that the goose is the woman of the house, the eagle is the invader. The difference is that while Helen's eagle took the woman from the house, Penelope's eagle destroyed both the woman and the house; not the building, the building is meaningless, but the entire *oikon*[33].

---

33 Immediately after dismissing the beggar's interpretation as too good to be true, she says that on "this ill-omened day" (literally, ill-*named*, δυσώνυμος) is coming something that will cut her off from "Odysseus's household" (Ὀδυσῆος οἴκου): she has relented to allow the contest of the 12 axes and marry the winner, forsaking "this house" (δῶμα =building, not oikos) which she will remember only in her dreams (ἔν περ ὀνείρῳ); which is "where" she described weeping and wailing after the eagle killed the geese (ἔν περ ὀνείρῳ). Much of this response mirrors the latent content of her dream. But she tells the beggar this in response to his agreement with the eagle that Odysseus is about to return. It is as if her response to the beggar is, "even if he comes back, it is too late." But it's only too late if she doesn't postpone the contest-- and she is not going to postpone it. Of course, the beggar enthusiastically endorses the contest

44

It is perhaps unsettling to imagine that we moderns have been fooled by an interpretation that couldn't even fool her. But the goal isn't to fool other people about her desires while she secretly harbors them; but to be told by an authority that she doesn't have them at all, that she desires something else. To be told what she believes, told what is true. The problem

---

anyway, as part of the dream's prophecy: don't worry, Odysseus will surely return. Penelope's response is strangely elaborate. What her response means is, "I wish you were right, by I doubt it." What she says, however, is this:

> If thou couldest but wish, stranger, to sit here in my halls and give me joy, sleep should never be shed over my eyelids. But it is in no wise possible that men should forever be sleepless, for the immortals have appointed a proper time for each thing upon the earth, the giver of grain. But I verily will go to my upper chamber and lay me on my bed, which has become for me a bed of wailings, ever bedewed with my tears, since the day when Odysseus went to see evil Ilios, that should never be named. There will I lay me down, but do thou lie down here in the hall...

Two sentences later, Athena pours sleep over her eyes.

This response is needlessly complicated except if taken literally: the "hall" she tells him to sleep in is the house (οἴκῳ); the "hall" she wishes he'd sit in is the same hall (μεγάροισι) as where the dream's dead geese were piled; "piled" here (ἐκέχυντο) is the same word she also chooses to explain sleep "pouring" over her (οὔ κέ μοι ὕπνος ἐπὶ βλεφάροισι χυθείη; both "pours" are χέω)-- distinctly different from the narrative explanation of sleep being *put on* her eyes by Athena (ἐπὶ βλεφάροισι βάλε) in 19.600.

45

is that this fails to work. The omnipotent eagle gives an interpretation. It is wrong, but more urgently for Penelope, it doesn't *take*. She then goes to the beggar asking for an interpretation, and he gives the same one. It doesn't take, either. In fact, after telling the dream to him-- likely because she spoke it to him, out loud-- her doubt is even greater. For her the dream is still open to interpretation. The defense has

---

But the grain-giving earth-- to what does that refer? An obvious guess would be the grain the geese were eating in the dream; but the geese's grain is πυρὸν while here "the giver of grain" is ζείδωρον ἄρουραν, an honorific for earth commonly used in the Odyssey. πυρὸν's association must lie elsewhere.

This brings us back to the eagle's piling the geese in the hall-- why did it do this? Surely it must be a foreshadowing of 22.385, where the narrative uses "piled" to describe what Odysseus does with the dead wooers. Did the dream prophesy even the location of the final pile of suitors (despite that the geese aren't suitors)? But unlike modern movies involving prophetic dreams, in which real life particulars finally align with the dream elements, Homeric dreams and prophesies align by similes and metaphors-- by words. These wooers' bodies are indeed described as piled, but

> like fishes that fishermen have drawn forth in the
> meshes of their net from the grey sea upon the
> curving beach, and they all lie heaped upon the
> sand, longing for the waves of the sea, and the
> bright sun takes away their life; even so now the
> wooers lay heaped upon each other.

It's an odd comparison, given that we are already primed for a comparison to a pile of dead geese-- and the fish in this comparison are still alive, to be killed by the sun (Ἥλιος). In 12.385, after receiving the news from "long robed" Lampetie that his flock has been killed by Odysseus's disobedient men, Helios asks Zeus for vengeance. Zeus agrees:

46

failed. She is in danger of knowing her wish.

᾽Ηέλι᾽, ἥ τοι μὲν σὺ μετ᾽ ἀθανάτοισι φάεινε καὶ
θνητοῖσι βροτοῖσιν ἐπὶ ζείδωρον ἄρουραν... Helios,
you shine on the immortals and the mortals on the
grain giving earth...

Zeus lets the men feast on the flock for 6 days (Odysseus lets the suitors
feast for 5 days) then on day 7 lures them into the sea where he suddenly
thunderbolts the men's ship-- not killing them directly, but casting them
into the sea, amidst the "sulphurous" smoke (ἐν δὲ θεείου πλῆτο); the
same sulphur and fire Odysseus requests of the old Eurycleia to purify the
house after killing the suitors (Εὐρύκλεια[v]: οἶσε θέειον, γρηῦ, κακῶν
ἄκος, οἶσε δέ μοι πῦρ).

The comparison between the future real events of 22.385 and the past real
events of 12.385 is Odysseus's wish, between the killed men *of* Odysseus
and the killed wooers *by* Odysseus: like men cast into water or fish cast
out of water, killed for consuming another's flock. But Homer has made a
different association for Penelope's dream: πυρὸν and πῦρ, grain and fire;
and her final words to the beggar have a different connotation: since you
wish my husband's return, I wish that you would burn in the hall with the
rest of the house.

She soon has another dream. NB she does not go to the beggar for its
interpretation.

47

The Wish That Must Not Be Named

It is generally known that Freud made a distinction between the latent wish and its distortion into the manifest content of the dream. Unfortunately, what is not as well known, even by those who should well know better, is Freud's distinction between the latent wish of the dream and the mechanism of that dream distortion. The mechanism of distortion is caused not by the dream's latent wish, but by *another* unconscious wish. It is this second wish that is more often sexual, not the latent wish of the dream, which is routinely non-sexual. Consider the foundational dream of "Irma's injection", in which Freud dreamt of a patient whose treatment had failed. Freud concluded that the latent wish was that his colleague Fleiss (and by extension, himself) was blameless in the treatment failure of his real life patient named Irma[34]. But the mechanism of this dream's distortion

---

34 In fact, this is not Freud's interpretation; this is what many writings about Freud's interpretation say he said was his interpretation. You may observe that this latent wish is hardly unacceptable, hardly requiring repression. What Freud wrote was that the dream "represented a particular state of affairs... that I was not responsible for the persistence of Irma's pains, *but that Otto was...*". Even this is not his wish but the *fulfillment* of his wish; Freud's astutely detected the latent *wish* that needed to be repressed: "...Otto had annoyed me by his remarks about (real life) Irma's

was primarily condensation, in which single elements of the dream took on multiple disparate associations (NB more often semantic than symbolic, e.g. the injection's "solution" (*lösung*) associated to the psychoanalytic "solution" (*lösung*) that Freud had offered the real life Irma that failed to cure her). The condensation of "solution" suggests that "Irma" was also a condensation of real life Irma and *multiple other women* he wished would adore him.

For a wish to require repression, it must be something one is not *allowed* to want, generally reinforced by guilt and the *fantasy* of paternal wrath. Explicit, real world punishments, by consequence, have the effect of removing unconscious repression; guilt is gone, even if there may still be explicit shame. In this way, lusting after another man (or 108 men) would not require repression because she *can* want the men[35]; lust may require suppression or discretion but hardly repression, and unwisely acting on that lust has a

---

incomplete (psychoanalytic) cure and the dream gave me my revenge by throwing the reproach back on him." (SE IV, p. 118-9). To duck blame even when you are to blame is hardly a wish that needs repression; but the primitive rage of blaming someone who knows you are to blame is precisely the kind of wish Freud would not want manifested.

35 It is notable that so many readings, not only psychoanalytic, detected a "repressed" wish for one or more of the suitors; but not because of any particular merit of the suitors, physical, emotional, or even Oedipal, but due to the prolonged celibacy. While this has a certain narrative logic to it, what happens most commonly to one with obsessive traits (even her bed is rooted to the ground) is that prolonged celibacy leads to sublimation; the sexual drive is turned towards some other *re*-productive outlet (art, children, health (whether wellness or hypochondriasis), etc) that maintains the status quo.

paternal-istic and public punishment. (Getting away with it, however, could result in repression and the return of the repressed in the form of symptoms.) By comparison, one is not allowed to "desire one's mother"-- yet beyond shame there are no explicit punishments-- so the mere thought comes with the fantasy of paternal wrath, and is thus repressed and returns as something else.

What are Penelope's dream's mechanisms of dream distortion-- which is the same question as, what are her primary mechanisms of unconscious defense? She displays the use of metonymy and portmanteau, both which move but do not obliterate meaning; at the loom and in the dream she displays undoing, a defense used to protect psychic homeostasis and return to the way things were; she does not choose a suitor but neither does she choose to dispatch them-- she makes no choice; she neither returns to her father's house nor takes full control of her own. Her dream has three distinct episodes, but they do not move the story forward, they obsessively recapitulate, dwell in the same moment, moving meanings around; and then the geese return-- it starts all over. *All of these are defenses against change.* They attempt to delay the inevitable, to undo Fate. But the desire that has been repressed isn't a return to life before the war-- this obvious desire would hardly need to be repressed. This is no grieving widow who keeps her husband's belongings the way they were before he left, maintaining the status quo ante bellum; what she wants unchanged is the status quo *post* bellum-- the status quo after the war ended and everyone else has returned. In this status quo she makes no choice-- does not choose a suitor or no suitor, or choose to wait for her husband or to mourn her husband. She certainly does not "move on", repaint the house and get new furniture. Neither does she fetishistically keep her husband alive by making a museum of the house or ritual visits to the cliff to see if white-sail boats return. She does the opposite, stretches out the state of his absence indefinitely by leaving it all to slowly increasing entropy, not in shambles but in decay, the house, the father in law, the handmaidens, all the way down to the dog.

The Second Dream

That night she has a second dream. She dreamt that she was laying beside a man who looked like Odysseus did when he first left for Troy, and she was so happy that she (in the dream) thought the dream was real.

The obvious interpretation is that what would make Penelope happy is Odysseus back in her bed. What should now be clear is that this cannot be the correct interpretation because this is literally the manifest content of the dream.

To whom does she go to interpret this dream? One chooses an interpreter with the authority to declare the meaning as if it was based on omniscience; but actual omniscience risks that the authority detects the correct interpretation. Telling the dream to the beggar is too risky in both directions; she already suspects he misinterpreted the first dream, but worse, he did not have the authority to make an interpretation true for her. So she goes to a higher omnipotent entity: god. It is useful to clarify the precise order of events: after having resigned herself to the bow contest[36]

---

36 It has been a source of considerable discussion how the contest would work, exactly through what part of the 12 axes was the arrow supposed to pass? In a psychoanalysis, so much focus on a comparatively trivial target would be interrogated as a diversion, a defense, against asking a more important question: why were they using a bow at all? And why was the

with the beggar's encouragement, she went to her chamber (19.600) with the handmaidens, crying out loud over Odysseus (κλαῖεν ἔπειτ᾽ Ὀδυσῆα, φίλον πόσιν), until she fell into pleasant sleep ἐπὶ βλεφάροισι βάλε γλαυκῶπις Ἀθήνη-- that Athena poured in her eyes. She later (20.59) awakens, and cries profusely. She then prays to Artemis to kill her

---

bow at home? Shouldn't he have taken it to war? But we are told he *never* took it on war trips, it was a memorial to Iphitus. So Odysseus's bow was not Odysseus's *weapon*-- in fact, what the Odyssey makes *explicitly* clear is that his main weapons were cunning and wisdom; surely a contest of wits would be more appropriate, riddles at dawn? It should be noted that a bow was sometimes even considered a "cowardly" weapon (though the Iliad describes entire units of archers, and praises them) and anyway would not be suitable for close quarters, hand-to-hand battles, except that is precisely what he "bravely" uses it for in Book 20, inside his house (managing to kill about 40 men with it before switching to the spear). Yes, he had taken all the suitors' weapons-- except for the 12 axes planted in the ground that any of the remaining 107 suitors could smash his head with. Knife beats gun under 21 feet; God help you if you brought a bow.

The bow test is typically understood to be a test of strength; yet the most common explanation for the mechanics of the contest is that the arrow is supposed to pass through some small hole in the axe, perhaps the hole in the handle where they could be hung on a wall (as in 21.421? But 19.54 Odysseus says he's shooting "through the iron") or through the coronal hole in the axe head when the handle is removed. However, then this contest becomes one of aim, of technical skill, even though the contest discusses the strength needed to string the bow (e.g. Amphimedon in Hades (24.170) says he and the other suitors lacked the strength (δύναμις)) and it still leaves the axes intact as projectiles available for suitors' self-defense.

A simple solution to this is that the arrow was to go physically through the axes (and thus destroy them); this explains the strength needed to shoot the bow, and justifies why *even* Telemachus was able to at least string it

53

(NB: shoot her with her bow; or be swept away like the famed orphaned virgins cared for by Aphrodite (NB right before their marriage)) so that she never pleases the heart[37] of a lesser man (20.92). In her prayer, she laments that though sleep can help you forget both the good and the bad, *nevertheless* (αὐτὰρ) in her case she's given bad dreams. *Then* she relates the dream.

---

three times yet still gave up (before being signaled by Odysseus not to try); as well as explaining the narrative's odd superfluous description of what would otherwise have been unremarkable: that the arrow was tipped with bronze (23.424). But in 19.574, she explains that these are the same axes Odysseus used to practice with, i.e. they are intact. We are left to conclude that while the narrative implies a test of strength, it is only a test of skill, a skill which any reasonably competent bowman might possess.

She mostly says this herself in 19.576 when first describing the contest, saying she will marry the winner-- not the one who succeeds, but the one who *most easily* (ῥηῐτατ) performs the feat.

Importantly, the contest was Penelope's idea, not Odysseus's (Amphimedon is wrong in 24.165, discussed later); it can be said that the cunning idea of pitting the suitors against each other was Penelope's weapon. Yet she chose a contest of skill or strength which many people could complete, and excluded the very trait that most distinguishes Odysseus-- his wiles. The contest she has chosen in no way *validly* or *reliably* tests for Odysseus, or even the best suitor. In fact, there is reason to believe she chose the bow believing that it *will not* distinguish Odysseus from any other man.

Even close readers of the Odyssey can misremember a key fact about the beggar: the suitors didn't want him to take a turn, not because he was just a beggar who could never succeed but because he was just a beggar *yet might succeed.* Penelope intervenes, saying let him try, it is quite unlikely-- not that he would succeed, she concedes he has a good chance-- but unlikely that such a beggar would want to marry her. The logical conclusion is that it doesn't matter who can do it, all suitors are the same to her, and she is resigned to her fate.

54

The obvious assumption is that it was a "bad dream" because she awoke to find it was not true. Yet no one would describe a happy dream as "bad" because it wasn't real, any more than one would call a nightmare "good" because one awakens to find it wasn't.

But the narrative leaves open the crucial possibility: does she think the beggar will succeed because she suspects he is Odysseus?

When precisely did she recognize him as her husband has been a subject of much discussion. But if one believes that she suspects the beggar is Odysseus, and this is why she advocated so strongly for him to have his turn, then one must contend with the terrible consequences of the very next line: she says if the beggar did succeed, she would reward him food, money, and *send him off.* This is an amazing response no matter what she suspects: she agrees to marry the winner of the contest, yet in advance negates the possibility that she would marry the winner of the contest, *especially* her husband. Perhaps this is a contest of wiles after all, and she plans to win.

37 Fagles: "Never let me warm the heart of a weaker man." μηδέ τι χείρονος ἀνδρὸς ἐϋφραίνοιμι νόημα. Fagles's word choice is interesting: ἐϋφραίνοιμι (εὐφραίνω, to please) is derived from φρήν which refers to the heart, but there is no Greek for Fagles's "warm" (Murray translates this phrase "gladden the heart"). In Penelope's dream, the Greek says it "warms" her to look on the geese (καί τέ σφιν ἰαίνομαι εἰσορόωσα); but there Fagles removes the "warm" and translates it to "I love to watch them all." It must be assumed Fagles saw and knew ἰαίνομαι; it thus appears he deleted it from where it actually is, and put it to where it isn't. This is displacement in its technical sense: the key to the maneuver is that even though this meaning has been given to the new target, the meaning belongs to *both* locations; displacement duplicates meaning, it does not eradicate or shift meaning. "Unresolved anger" can be displaced from the father to the husband and carried into marriage, but the father isn't consequently absolved. Thus, the Greek word ἰαίνομαι=warms is still there referring to the geese; but now there's an English word "warm"

But even a nightmare has beneath it a wish fulfillment[38]. Note the strange phrasing: why in the dream does the man look *like* Odysseus (εἴκελος αὐτῷ)? And why in the *manifest dream* is her heart *nevertheless* (αὐτὰρ) pleased? In the manifest dream it looks like she got what she *didn't* want-- Odysseus's return-- nevertheless she was happy, because it's *not* Odysseus. Not-- as in negation. It is neither the man before he left nor the man who may return; it is the man who left only, the man *as* gone. She wants to be with him as absent. The status quo post bellum.

She tells the dream to omnipotent Artemis; like the beggar, Artemis is theoretically omniscient but whose practical value is in her power to declare what the dream means. But usefully, unlike the beggar and exactly like a god, Artemis is not going to say anything; so the prayer spoken to Artemis becomes to Penelope Artemis's confirmation of the prayer. She told Artemis what the dream obviously means, which is felt reflexively as Artemis confirming what it means.

The second defensive maneuver of the dream is to make it "feel real," as if the intensity of the dream stood for the intensity of the wish. But intensity of a dream element is

---

regarding the suitors after the second dream. For Fagles, therefore, who knows Greek and English, both meanings are now *literally* present. This is his, not Penelope's, association between the geese and suitors.

38 According to Freud, the nightmare's fear and anxiety derive not from the latent content, but from some incidental real-life anxiety that distorts the *manifestation* of the wish fulfillment into a nightmare. In this case, the likely daytime anxiety was the confluence of the beggar's failure to save her from her first dream, and the impending contest.

inversely related to the success of distortion, such that very vivid or obvious symbols are almost always not what they appear to be (consider nightmares or phobic elements, or overtly sexual dreams), chosen to make the dreamer think they "know" what they mean, and prevent deeper reflection; while hazy or even forgotten aspects of the dream are the last ditch defenses of an unsuccessfully distorted latent wish. Note also the eagle's interpretation begins, "not a dream, but a happy waking vision, real as day..." The intuitions are clear and distinct, nothing could be hidden; so why would anyone go any deeper?

Is The Purpose Of The Penelope Subplot To Show Her As A Model Of Fidelity?

Penelope's latent wish for the destruction of her household and Odysseus not to return contradicts the apparent general purpose of the subplot, which is to show Penelope as the heroic model of wifely fidelity, nobly resisting the suitors and keeping hope in her heart for her husband's return. This has been the conventional understanding. But if showing her fidelity were the purpose of the story, then she would just be faithful. Instead, the story subverts this in several important ways.

Fidelity To One's Desire

The first is that she tells the suitors she'll marry one if they'd only wait until she finishes weaving a burial shroud for her father-in-law; at night she undoes the weaving that she did in the day. This goes on for almost four years.

Certainly this ruse preserves her fidelity. But if her fidelity is her duty, why can't she just refuse to marry anyone, out of fidelity? How does *not choosing* but instead keeping them around yet passively tricking everybody make her more honorable? The only way this makes sense is if she was in some way obligated to remarry, such that in order to *avoid* her duty and instead remain faithful, she plays this trick. Her faithfulness might then have value because she is *not* supposed to be faithful. This is perhaps a defensible view, but it would require her subplot to be understood not as pro-fidelity but antisocial; not "do the right thing, be faithful to your husband" but rather "never mind what's right, do what you want."

Even so, her unweaving uncovers a plot hole: she took four years to do what everyone would have known takes less than a month, and, at least on that loom, no other weaving could be done. This suggests the episode is less a realistic plot event and more of a thematic metaphor for her "wiles" through "handiwork" (e.g. Antinous's description of her in 2.110)-- a metaphor for her strategy for producing a desired outcome. Except weaving was *already* an explicit textual metaphor for "women's work" (e.g. 1.355 *and* 23.350); therefore, the weaving/unweaving isn't something she does to produce a desired outcome, but how she remains unproductive, avoiding her obligations as a woman; how she avoids action, maintaining the status quo. It is *undoing*. She's not choosing a result, she is avoiding the choice.

But some of her servants (NB: she uses the plural) reveal her ploy to the suitors. Why would they do this? It might be worth the betrayal to gain favor with the future master of the house, but until that marriage they would risk the punitive whims of Penelope. A more textually supported explanation is that while Penelope delays action at the loom, the suitors are acting on, i.e. raping, the servant girls[39]. Perhaps self-protection drove the servants to betray their mistress. Not simply being raped; the situation Penelope has orchestrated forces a stark dichotomy: while the servants have shamelessly chosen to be raped, Penelope gets to pretend she chose to avoid it. If Odysseus returns-- or even if anyone becomes master of the house-- the fallen women are very likely to be killed for shaming the house by being complicit in their own rape, which is indeed what brutally happens-- by Telemachus, no less, who in a solid example of displacement punished the women for what he was responsible to protect them from. What does this show us? Penelope's fidelity is on the backs of her slaves, and their necks.

Why would an unfinished burial shroud postpone a wedding? The reasonable answer is that as the wife of a new man, she would not be expected, or even permitted, to weave for her former father-in-law. Penelope explains that the other women would shame her if she left a wealthy man to die without a shroud. (No such shame in leaving poor women to suffer for her.) This sounds noble, except Penelope says this noblesse knowing her plan was to *not* finish the shroud. Certainly this delays having to choose; but to understand the purpose of the weaving, we must take the story literally;

---

39 Interesting that Amphimedon says a (singular) woman (καὶ τότε δή τις ἔειπε γυναικῶν 24.145) revealed her deception, but Penelope says it was the (plural) "slaves" (καὶ τότε δή με διὰ δμῳάς 19.140). Penelope here blames the victims, as a class. These "reckless bitches" (κύνας οὐκ ἀλεγούσας) whom Penelope may have condemned to rape are not to her at all linked to the "fair tressed Achaean women" in the dream (who indeed raped) who attended to her grief.

Amphimedon in Hades (24.146) explicitly describes the consequence of Penelope finishing the radiant[40] shroud: "and then, *therefore*" (καὶ τότε δή[41]) Odysseus was brought back. The weaving/unweaving prevented her choosing a husband, but at the same time doing and undoing the possibility of her

---

[40]Another unfortunate mistranslation: not "radiant" like Helen's "radiant" goose (ἀργὴν), but "shone like the sun and the moon" (ἠελίῳ ἐναλίγκιον ἠὲ σελήνῃ)-- a phrase with a different verb (ἠελίου αἴγλη πέλεν ἠὲ σελήνης) used elsewhere to describe what appeared over the glorious house of Menelaus (4.45) and over the palace of Alcinous. (7.84) Note the commonality: men in disguise are sent by Athena to the homes of men with honored wives (Helen 4.305: δῖα γυναικῶν "divine of women"; Arete (7.70) οἵ μίν ῥα θεὸν "as a god") --women honored above all other women not per se for something they have done, but because under their husbands they have an *oikon* (Arete: γυναῖκες ὑπ᾽ ἀνδράσιν οἶκον ἔχουσιν (7.69)).

[41] καὶ τότε δή ῥ᾽ Ὀδυσῆα κακός ποθεν ἤγαγε δαίμω, i.e. apodotic. Bakker references Chafe (1994: 63-64) and, while not describing this passage specifically, claims that phrases like καὶ τότε δή (=and then) "regulate the flow of discourse rather than being part of it." There are numerous examples of this throughout the Odyssey, but it cannot be true here. The phrasing, intensity, and conviction with which Amphimedon laments the trickery of Penelope can only make sense if the return of Odysseus is *logically implied* by the completion of the robe. Consider 7.140, in which Athena has wrapped Odysseus in a mist:

> ἀμφὶ δ᾽ ἄρ᾽ Ἀρήτης βάλε γούνασι χεῖρας Ὀδυσσεύς,
> καὶ τότε δή ῥ᾽ αὐτοῖο πάλιν χύτο θέσφατος ἀήρ.

> Around Arete's knees Odysseus put his hands, καὶ τότε δή the divinely-cast mist dissolved.

In this example καὶ τότε δή, "and then", does not assert a material cause/effect relationship between the two events (it is not Odysseus that makes the mist dissolve by his actions) but neither is it simply

61

actual husband coming back[42]. It was the obsessive ritual of one attempting to maintain the status quo. Of course only the obsessive believes this will work. But more specifically, the obsessive believes that the ritual is *necessary but not sufficient* to prevent the undesired outcome; the ritual might not succeed, but if she stops the ritual the undesired event is

---

coincidence; it is rather a rule of inference:

> [Proposition: if Odysseus put his hands on Arete, then the Mist would dissolve.]
>
> He put his hands on Arete
>
> καὶ τότε δή the Mist dissolved (modus ponens).

What we can know from this proposition is that putting his hands on her is sufficient for the mist to dissolve; but if he does NOT put his hands on her, we can not assume any outcome. Similarly, if we see the mist is dissolved, we cannot assume it was Odysseus; the logic allows for other possible ways for the mist to dissolve (e.g. the will of god); but if we see the mist is not dissolved, then we can infer he did not put his hands on her.

With respect to the shroud, and more formally:

> [If the shroud is COMPLETED then Odysseus RETURNS] (1)
>
> The shroud is COMPLETED
>
> καὶ τότε δή Odysseus RETURNS

The specific power of this logical formulation is revealed when we grasp the *use* of Penelope's weaving/unweaving: it is a ritual-- it is not a magic spell. Performing a ritual does not guarantee a desired outcome (the inverse of (1) is not equivalent); but NOT performing it guarantees the outcome does occur. In Penelope's case, the ritual was the weaving/unweaving, for the purpose of preventing Odysseus from returning. ONLY IF she performs the ritual, will he NOT return.

The psychic purpose of the ritual is logically consistent with

62

logically guaranteed.

Staging Of The Other's Desire

The second subversion of her heroic fidelity is that Athena *causes* Penelope to appear more attractive to the suitors (18.190 πάσσονα θῆκεν ἰδέσθαι), in the same

---

Amphimedon's statement, (1), above.

> If NOT RETURNS then NOT COMPLETED (contrapositive of (1))   (2)
>
> NOT COMPLETED= PERFORMING ritual of weaving/unweaving   (3)
>
> IF NOT RETURNS then PERFORMING ritual of weaving/unweaving. (4)

We see here that PERFORMING the ritual guarantees nothing:

> PERFORMING
>
> therefore NOT RETURNS

is the fallacy of affirming the consequent in (4).   The logically valid conclusion is what is implied if she did NOT PERFORM the ritual:

> NOT PERFORMING
>
> therefore NOT NOT RETURNS=RETURNS (modus tollens of (4), and equivalent to 1)

One might ask how we can know that for Penelope, the ritual of unweaving/weaving is to keep Odysseus away, instead of, say, not

63

way/language Athena enhanced Odysseus to Nausicaa (7.84) and later to Penelope (23.155)[43]. Athena makes her more desirable to them, so that they "all pray to go to bed with her" (18.214). But Penelope gets more than a makeover: Athena also makes Penelope *want* to show off for the suitors, want to entice them (18.159). How would this increase the value of her fidelity? If her attractiveness increased the pursuits of the

---

realizing that all she had to do to *magically* bring him home was finish the shroud. Importantly, the weaving/unweaving is already established textually as a delay, an undoing: symmetrically (i.e. displacement), the ritual is already for the purpose of preventing marriage to the suitors. Structurally, the difference is that a magic spell is *sufficient* for a good outcome (or to avoid a bad outcome): if SPELL then OUTCOME; while a ritual is *necessary* for a good outcome (or to avoid a bad outcome): if OUTCOME then RITUAL. In practice, it is relatively simple to ask the person whether the ritual or spell is necessary or whether it is merely sufficient, e.g. if you don't do this, what will happen? The ritual does not guarantee results, but it is absolutely necessary, there is a 100% catastrophe rate without it. A spell is sufficient-- it is 100% effective-- but not necessary, things might still turn out ok. A ritual is strongly suggested when the consequence that results from not performing it is described as a subjective catastrophe, e.g. "I may as well be dead!"

In this way, what are popularly called "rituals" may not be rituals but spells; and modern medicines may be *thought of by the patient* as rituals or spells depending on their perceived logical relationship to an outcome.

The important distinct usage of καὶ τότε δή as a kind of inference rule and not as a merely stylistic apodosis can be further illustrated by the situations in which the *English* translation is *erroneously* "and then", to create a modus ponens inference-- e.g. 20.89 Penelope's second dream, "[Odysseus lay by my side] *and then* my heart was glad". One might expect the Greek here is καὶ τότε δή, i.e. "if he returns, then her heart would be glad"-- but Homer does not use καὶ τότε δή but a countervalenced word: αὐτὰρ, *nevertheless*. The Greek says quite the opposite of the English.

64

suitors, then the scene is less about remaining true to Odysseus and more about getting credit for maintaining his house (i.e. herself)-- something she has failed to do with all the rest of the house, down to his dog. A common way to dismiss the scene is to say it represents her desire, that she enjoys being lusted after by these men. Unfortunately for this

---

42 Note the structure of the undoing. The rigorous definition of undoing is to undo something that has already occurred. Thus, the purpose of her weaving and unweaving is in fact to undo not (just) the future marriage to a suitor, but her past marriage to Odysseus-- to prevent him from returning and they being a couple. NOT performing the undoing ritual means the marriage is not undone-- they are "still" married, and he returns. But not wanting her husband to return is obviously an unacceptable wish. The defense against this unacceptable wish is *declaring*-- having an other declare-- that the weaving/unweaving is for the *purpose* of preventing her marriage to the suitors. It is indeed for that purpose, but so could a dozen other maneuvers, such as picking an arbitrary wedding date 4 years in the future. But 108 suitors have been fooled into declaring it was to delay a future marriage to them *only*; it's conscious, deliberate purpose paralleled its unconscious purpose, and also served as a defense against this unconscious desire being detected.

43 And, interestingly, Laertes to Odysseus (24.365): καὶ πάσσονα θῆκεν ἰδέσθαι. What seems to make Penelope's "enhancement" remarkable is that she is the only woman who gets enhanced. Murray translates the phrase as "statelier to behold", but πάσσονα has a decidedly masculine connotation, literally "thicker", i.e. more muscular. Fagles translates the phrase for Laertes as "his build [was made] more massive" but for Penelope tries "fuller in form to all men's eyes". Perhaps the implication is they were poorly nourished, but the next line after Penelope is made longer limbed, meatier, and whiter, is the approach of the "white-armed" handmaidens. The implication is youthfulness, vigor, desirability. But is there a deeper commonality that would justify the repetition of the phrase that is otherwise awkwardly applied to a woman, and not simply say that she was made more beautiful? Unlike Penelope, the men who are made

perspective, the text has her emphasize that she loathes the suitors. Even if we rely on the projection that women of her times reflexively derived some satisfaction out of being desired by desirable men, it is very unlikely *she* derived any satisfaction out of being desired by *those* men[44].

But taken more literally, what Athena has changed is that the suitors are now attracted to Penelope, whereas before they were attracted to the house. In this way, Penelope's fidelity suddenly takes on an important valence: her previous fidelity didn't count because they didn't really want *her*, but now they do. This is why it will bring "greater honor to her husband" (18.155). Perhaps no different from modern fidelity, what counts is not that she deprives herself of the others, but that she deprives the others of herself.

Rivalry Over a Prize

The third subversion in the Odyssey is something even less realistic than the existence of a Cyclops, and that is the presence of the suitors at all. Under whose *authority* are they allowed to court her, let alone eat her food? Patriarchy or no,

---

more masculine all know it is only an illusion (and in Laertes's case, Odysseus observing knows it also.) Penelope, however, does not know that it is an illusion-- but the reader does, because her enhancement has a modifier: she is enhanced while she *sleeps*, to become "whiter than *sawn ivory*"-- cf 19.560, a dream-- a deception that brings no fulfillment.

44 The expensive question for the psychology of the reader is: does becoming more beautiful make her want to show off? There is no universal answer, of course, but each individual's answer reveals more about the individual than Penelope. But Homer spares us the self-reflection: *first* she wanted to show off, and *then* she was enhanced.

she is a queen and the highest ranking member of the house, and even the implicit structure of Achaean patriarchy still required the presence of an explicit patriarch. Penelope's marriage to Odysseus was negotiated for her, as was Helen's to Menelaus; suitors arrived under regulated traditions and marriage was ultimately a negotiation between fathers. But no one consults Icarius, and Laertes is with the dog. Unless we propose that it is, in fact, the "structural patriarchy" that implicitly gives the suitors the privilege (not even the right) of being in the home to court her, then Penelope retains the right to expel them all. Yet she doesn't. The counter is that the absence of an explicit patriarch is precisely why the suitors have the power to be there (i.e. they can do whatever they have the physical power to do, since nothing greater than them obstructs them)-- and certainly this is the logic they use to rape the servant girls or plan to kill Telemachus; but in fact they do not *at all* do what they want to do, because they spend four years not fighting each other, not taking over the house, and waiting for Penelope to choose. Even when they discover they've been tricked, all they do is force her to *choose*. Evidently, there is a power greater than 108 noblemen combined, and it is Penelope.

Yet after four years of aggressive auditioning no leading man is identifiable, and NB these are the best men, the sons of the noblemen. Traditionally suitors would come to the house and feed her, throw lavish feasts for her and her family and friends, show off their status and wealth-- if nothing else beat her or each other in a footrace-- to entice her to marry them. For twenty years no one has done this, and for four years they all do the opposite-- it only occurs to them to offer her gifts after she has been eroticized. It is as if they wanted to be indistinguishably undesirable[45]– to *her*.

The purpose of the ambivalent presence of the suitors-- present but not really engaged in competition for her-- is to show that there is no competition between suitors for her. The competition is between the suitors *and* her[46]. The prize is

---

45 It is telling that modern readers simply accept that under archaic patriarchy the suitors had the *right* to be there. No male in the story thinks this, certainly not the ranking patriarch Menelaus, nor any of the other kings, let alone Odysseus. The ancient patriarchy was only one layer in a hierarchy, it granted privileges, not rights; Penelope is not obligated to endure their presence. That they are not *allowed* to be there, and should be ashamed for being there, is not just a speculation but a textual assertion, e.g. 21.330, in which she asks Eurymachus why would he be ashamed if the beggar succeeds with the bow, when he doesn't worry about the shame of dishonoring and consuming the house of Odysseus.

46 This significant fact is easy to overlook in translation, but not only do the suitors act not as rivals but instead as a united brotherhood (e.g. against Telemachus), Homer has them call each other ἑταῖροι-- which can briefly be translated here "brothers in arms"-- several times (e.g. 16.350, 21.100, 21.140). Worthy of its own analysis, it is worth mentioning that the word hetairos (m) "brother in arms" evolved into the word hetaira (f) "courtesan/prostitute," and then was further abstracted to only mean courtesan. A possible link between the usages may be the sexual relationship inherent in "brothers in arms", e.g. hetairoi Achilles and Patroclus in the Iliad-- that continues to courtesans. But if this is the link, why was it sexual-- i.e. why did "hetairos" lose the martial (and gender) connotation but retain the sexual, and not the other way around? The Odyssey, "in between" the Iliad and Herodotus, offers a suggestion: what makes the suitors contemptible in their own right-- worse than women-- is that they retained the sexual relationship to each other but had lost the masculine martial spirit. They had become *decadent*. Thus, the purpose

68

the house. This may seem obvious, but she already has the house. She doesn't need to compete with them. The central dynamic in a rivalry between a subject and a rival over a prize is that the subject isn't really fighting for the prize; the desire is for the destruction of the rival. (The rival does not perceive a rivalry, the rival perceives it as fait accompli.)

In this case, to destroy the rival isn't her desire, but Odysseus's, which has become hers. But the rivalry also benefits the subject because it gives the subject a stable identity. As long as she doesn't choose a suitor and her husband doesn't return, she maintains the identity she has had the longest, the very identity that we see even 3000 years later: a homebound wife marking time, surrounded by unchosen possibilities, wishing her husband would return.

---

of the evolution of the word to female courtesans was in order to use it as an insult against men who had the trappings of hetairoi (sex, a spear) but lacked the substance (love, fights). Even if Penelope had wanted to sleep with them, she could not have wanted to marry them.

What Does A Husband Want A Faithful Wife For?

Of course, a fairly conventional "unconventional" interpretation of the Penelope/suitors subplot is that Penelope secretly desired the suitors. If true, does this undermine her fidelity? It is illustrative to follow the logic to the end. Before Athena made Penelope desirable to them, the prize (for the suitors) was the house. It follows that her fidelity to the house did not require her to abstain from sex with them-- only from marrying them, and losing the house. In reaction to the Homeric tradition that Penelope was heroically faithful, a remarkable later version declared that Penelope had willingly slept with all 108 of the suitors. No doubt the purpose of this version, written after the Golden Age had passed and therefore in adolescent reaction to not inheriting any of its gold, was to tear down the previous generation's shibboleths; cheapen the iconic Penelope, and even downgrade their grandparents' idol to an oblivious cuckold who naively believed his wife was faithful despite her *allowing* a hundred wealthy sportsmen to sleep near her. It is likely significant that the author of this particular story, the tyrant Duris of Samos, claimed to be a descendant of Alcibiades; the significance being not that he was indeed a descendant of Alcibiades, but that of all the people of 5th century Athens he could have pretended to be a descendant of, he chose Alcibiades. Nevertheless, it is not so textually preposterous that Penelope *may* have been unfaithful; her very own son in Book 1 muses out loud that a man can be sure of one's mother, but never of one's father. Turns out there are men who would kill for that kind of certainty.

But what makes Duris's fantasy inadvertently revealing isn't that she slept with all of the suitors; it is that she slept with *every single one* of the suitors. The form of this change is the conversion of multiple acts of behavior to a single act *about identity*[47] and absolves one of the significance of the

---

47 To grasp this specific way this is used as a psychic defense-- and what it reveals about the hierarchy of values to the user-- consider the set of losses from trading stocks. A man starts with $150, and loses $10, $20, $34, $36. Then he goes to lunch. He comes back and makes a final trade, and loses $50. There are several ways he can understand his day:

(1)	L= {10, 20, 34, 36, 50}	$|L|$= 6
(2)	L= {{10, 20, 30, 34, 36}, 50}	$|L|$= 2
(3)	L= {everything}	$|L|$= 1

(1) and (2) tell a story about *how* he lost the money: e.g. (1) says he lost more with every trade; (2) says he lost several times and then went all or nothing on the last trade. Professional traders record their day as both cases (1) and (2), because that is how they learn about their *behavior*. But the amateur trader has no desire to tell himself any story of how he lost-- or won-- the money, because despite saying *out loud* he wants to make money, the story that he really wants to tell is about *identity*: he is *a trader*. So (3) simply declares he lost all the money, or even that he lost $150. The amount of money he lost is less damning than the number of times he lost money. This justifies (to himself) his final bet of $50, it

71

consequences of the acts[48]. All of them is less than n of them[49]. Instead of being a woman used by men, she is a woman who uses men. It doesn't count[50].

Unfortunately for Duris, his story therefore ends up reinforcing her fidelity- to Odysseus. For example, Odysseus's split comments about the bed-- first bragging that

makes it much easier to lose it, because it will not increase the number of losses: it will still be *one*.

Note there is in the above sentence built-in a separate defense: "the amount of money he lost is less damning..." To whom? Imagine he tries to tell his wife (3). Suspicious, she presses him to learn how he lost the money, and is reluctantly told (1). She understands that (3) was the lie he told so she wouldn't think less of him: "he didn't want me to realize he's a terrible trader." If she says this *out loud*, he will shamefully admit it, perhaps even resent her for thinking so little of him; but this shame *is* the defense, because in that instant she has become (he has made her into) an omnipotent entity that has declared that, though terrible at it, he is in fact a trader. *And he will not change*. The "correct" maneuver for her would have been to argue about the money as money, but never say *out loud* the reason he lied, never refer to him as anything other than *husband*; thus, she cannot become the omnipotent entity he fooled into asserting he was a trader. But this is quite different from the maxim, "criticize the behavior, not the person" because even if the behavior is changed, the person remains free to self-identify. Unless he *becomes* a husband, it's only a matter of time before the trader trades again. Neither should she explicitly state he is "not a trader"-- revealing what she knows about him is can be easily misheard, misused, or dismissed: she doesn't know me at all. The best maneuver is to state what she desires him to be, and then he must choose.

To the wife, the losses are different, "$34" has a certain intrinsic value that counts more than "$10". But this is not the case with suitors. For Duris's *audience*, Penelope sleeping with Amphimedon is not different than with Antinous; neither is sleeping with every single one of them-- the suitors are a number, not a number of suitors. The only way sleeping with one

he made it so sturdy only a god could move it, but then musing, "I don't know if my bed is still firm in the ground, or if some man has already cut under the bottom of the olive tree and moved it..." (23.200)-- would seem to go from Homeric double entendre to Duric irony, except that by sleeping with all the suitors, no *individual* man moved the bed. Furthermore, in Duris's version what changes is that she sleeps with them, but what does not change is that she does *not* sleep with Odysseus-- because, she says, of her fear that she could be seduced. If (for Duris) she has already slept with suitors, then this seduction can only refer to *love*. She's entertained herself with casual infidelity, but when she meets

---

would be different from any other is if she only sleeps with some but not all-- she has distinguished between them in some way. Now the individual infidelities *count*.

48 See also Penelope's dream: "killed all the geese"-- here the number is rendered irrelevant because it is indeed irrelevant, it is one *act*.

49 There is a textual example of the difference. Odysseus executes the slave women who "shamed" his house. But he didn't kill all of them, only the shameful ones. Presumably, he would have killed all of them if they had all been shameful; but, applying the logic used with the suitors, he also would have killed all of the women if he didn't know which or even if they had been shameful. And no matter how bad the suitors are for being cads, he would have had to devise a lesser punishment for them if he knew which men were truly adulterers.

50 It raises the value of Penelope's sexuality, and therefore also Odysseus's, perhaps best exemplified by a 19th century joke, more explicit in the Russian, my sanitized translation here: "As your friend, I have to tell you something, but before I do I have a question: would you rather hear that your wife slept with all your friends; or that she tried to sleep with all your friends and failed, and one of them has to come tell you she's a nut?"

73

the man she suspects is her soulmate-- she makes him wait, prove himself. That sex is special. It is debatable how much this strategy would comfort a returning husband[51], but Duris's surreptitious distinction isn't for her husband but for the audience; its form inadvertently elevates her fidelity, the very thing he was trying to undermine with the content.

---

51 It is not entirely preposterous that it did comfort him. 23.345 describes the pillow talk in which Odysseus recounts to Penelope his adventures, including his time with Calypso. The details are not given, but it must be presumed that since he told her how long he was there, and that Calypso offered him immortality, and wanted to make him her husband, Penelope must have understood that he had had sex with her. Such sex could be dismissed as historically accepted male privilege but recounting it to the wife was not. It was demonstrably dangerous. (NB 1.430 explicitly tells us that Laertes didn't sleep with his slave Eurycleia because he was afraid of his wife!) The reveal makes sense, however, if the purpose of his admission is to prove that it doesn't count, because it was only sex.

But why prove anything? He could simply have not told her about Calypso. Unless he had been caught, why would a husband introduce a distinction between love and sex now? Because his wife already had. Recall what a page earlier has just happened between them: the "bed test" of 23.200. Odysseus has revealed himself, but laments Penelope won't accept it, so offers to sleep on the couch. Penelope seems to relent, "I know what kind of man you are", and tells Eurycleia to move the bed outside. He gets angry, because of course the bed can't be moved, it was built into a still planted olive tree trunk. This is something only she and he would know; he has passed the test, and Penelope's "knees were loosened where she sat and her heart melted". The double entendre would be almost salacious if it were not exactly wrong, because this is not why he passed the test, and is not why he gets angry, and this is not what he says. What he says is, "who [already] moved my bed elsewhere?" He says this in response to what Penelope had said, which was commanding Eurycleia to *prepare* the bed that he built himself that *is* outside the chamber. *It has already been moved*. This is why he is angry. The point was never that

74

Duris's version can be perhaps thought of as an attempt at justifying Odysseus's violent actions, but ironically reveals the limitations of Odysseus's ability to act. In the Homeric version, Penelope is faithful, but Odysseus kills all the suitors merely because they were shameful. It is perhaps excessive by modern standards, but one easily intuits the logic of

---

the bed could not be moved; of course it can be moved, he closes by explicitly saying he isn't sure if whether by now someone has *already* cut out beneath the stump and moved it. Neither is it a clever way to test if he had the secret knowledge about the bed, because had it in fact been moved, then everybody could know how it was made. It is not a test to prove his identity; it is a test of emotional response, *and his response was rage*. And as he spoke, Penelope's knees and heart respond revealingly-- but much different than the relieved/welcoming innuendo of the English, because the phrase "ὣς φάτο, τῆς δ᾽ αὐτοῦ λύτο γούνατα καὶ φίλον ἦτορ" is used almost exclusively as a *wretched admission of hopelessness*: e.g. Odysseus's "knees loosen and heart melts" when Poseidon sends the winds to destroy him (5.295); when he sees the suitors taking spears and armor from what should have been the locked in the storeroom; Penelope's "knees are loosened and heart melted" when she hears that the suitors plan to kill Telemachus (4.700); and the *entire* phrase starting with "as he spoke..." is used to describe Lycaon's submission when Achilles says he will kill him (Il 21.110). Lycaon was right; it was hopeless.

The phrase is, in its form, a "slip of the tongue": an accidental reveal that is quickly, and successfully, rescinded. Submission is quickly recast as relief. It is not until later in the Odyssey that the phrase is *perhaps* ever used to imply joy at reconnaissance, but we should interpret that (single) instance carefully. In psychoanalysis, future (yet correct) meanings of words, phrases, or symbols can be used to defend against a prior meaning; e.g. a person *usually* using "seldom" to mean "often", and then at some point begins to consistently use it only to mean "rarely"; the transition signals some accidental slip of the tongue in the past that needs to be forever obliterated. (A conscious example: a man's lover cancels their date, so he goes to dinner with his wife where he accidentally calls his

equivalence. If we follow Duris's version, Odysseus would be killing them because they were all truly adulterers. But it now becomes clear that he has the ability to kill all the suitors if she slept with *none* of them, or if she slept with *every single one* of them-- but he cannot kill them *all* if she slept with only *some* of them[52].

---

wife by his lover's pet name; from then on to deflect suspicion he continues to call his wife by that pet name.) In 24.345, Laertes tests Odysseus by asking him to tell him things only they would know (NB the much simpler test that Penelope didn't employ). Odysseus does, and "*his father's* knees loosened and heart melted". This likely is the recently invented meaning of the phrase-- it means what Odysseus wants it to mean for Laertes (NB: referred to has "his father"), which is the joy of reconnaissance. But the narration does not fully endorse this, nor eradicate its previous, literal/contextual meaning, which we should follow in sequence: Odysseus reveals himself to Laertes and tells him he has just killed all the insolent wooers. Laertes says: prove you are Odysseus. Odysseus then tells him some secret information. Then "his father's" knees and heart give out, and he faints. Well, did he faint from sentence #1 or #2? He awakens, and the first thing Laertes says is that he has great dread that all the suitors' families will descend on them.

If context and consistency should guide the interpretation of the phrase, consider that Laertes is then given a hot bath and compliments on his new physique, and his response is that he wishes he was younger/stronger τῷ κε σφέων γούνατ᾽ ἔλυσα-- then he himself would have loosened the knees of the suitors.

A final example: "Knees loosened and heart melted" seems to be used in a sexual sense in 18.214, describing the suitors gazing on enhanced Penelope:

> ... the knees of the wooers were loosened and their
> hearts enchanted with love, and they all prayed,

76

It may thus be a fact that Penelope was faithful, or at least faithful in the more important aspect of love, but given the subversions it cannot be true that the purpose of the Penelope subplot is to show this.

If she didn't want the suitors around, why didn't she just

---

each that he might lie by her side.

Murray likely hoped to draw a parallel between the suitors' sexual desire here with Penelope's in 23.200 by translating both phrases using the same words. But while the Greek makes the "knees loosening" identical (τῶν δ᾽ αὐτοῦ λύτο γούνατ᾽) unlike Penelope the suitors' hearts were not melted, or even enchanted: their souls were *bewitched* ἔρῳ δ᾽ ἄρα θυμὸν ἔθελχθεν. This is Athena's doing; as much as "laying" with Penelope might be enjoyable, the phrase indicates their powerlessness against Athena.

Another peculiarity of Penelope's "test" of Odysseusness needs explanation. Why suggest the bed be moved at all? As a test of secret knowledge, she could simply have asked him to describe the bed. Why move it outside the "bedchamber", *thalamon*, θάλαμον?

Θάλαμος is used frequently by narration to describe such private bedchambers (not just Penelope's, but also Telemachus's, etc); and Odysseus means it here as such; but the only time the word θάλαμον is spoken *out loud* is in order to refer to Odysseus's private treasure storeroom (e.g. Telemachus 19.15, 22.155; Eumaeus 22.165; Odysseus 19.285.) Crucially, Penelope herself only uses θάλαμον to refer to this storeroom (19.255) saying *out loud* she once gave Odysseus a tunic (=shroud) she had stored there-- *and she says it to Odysseus*. Whatever the word θάλαμος means, it is only used for one purpose, especially by her. If we take her literally, the bed is with the other treasures of his house, Odysseus is welcome to them, and she consents to be one of his stored treasures. But-- and for her unfortunately-- Odysseus wants the bed and what he means by thalamos-- his bedchamber. He wants her as

tell them to leave? She *could* have. She did not. It's such a basic point that it sandwiches the entire Odyssey, this very question explicitly stated by Antinous in the beginning and dead Amphimedon at the end. Amphimedon thinks it was all an elaborate plot, keeping them around *so that* she could kill them. But Amphimedon is wrong[53], her wish is not to kill them or to get rid of them, nothing she does in life or in her dreams suggests this.

It is certainly something Odysseus wants. Perhaps the entire subplot's purpose is to show all of the things Odysseus wants.

---

wife.

Penelope's test was not to find out who he was, but to find out what she was, to him: treasure, or wife? His anger at the moved bed-- the logic that if the bed could be moved now then it had already been moved-- meant he was being offered her/the bed the way the other men had had it, as treasure, as a prize. It was her final attempt to maintain the status quo post bellum. But that's not what he wants. He responds with rage. She submits. Lycaon was right.

52 There is a psychic maneuver that could be employed to kill all the suitors even if only some were adulterous, though it breaks the story. Recall that Odysseus did not kill all the handmaids, only the ones that had sex with the suitors. But in fact, Odysseus didn't kill them at all-- he had Telemachus do it, i.e. a possible solution would have been to kill the adulterous suitors himself, and leave the rest to Telemachus. But then it acknowledges that Penelope is selectively unfaithful, i.e. then the cheating counts, and her character's purpose in the greater story (discussed below) is nullified.

53 Formally wrong: while getting rid of them, killing them, or marrying them are very different acts, they are still formally all acts; and the form of Penelope's behavior in the story is not to act on her desires.

If we compare the structure of Penelope's dream to the structure of the Odyssey itself, then both the first part of the dream (up until the eagle returns) and the first part of the Odyssey (including up until the eagle returns) is Penelope's wish. All of the rest of the Odyssey that follows-- the eagle's return and interpretation, Odysseus's secret return, killing the suitors and reclaiming his house-- mirrors the second part of the dream (the eagle's return and interpretation), and thus more closely represents what (she thinks) Odysseus wants[54].

But why would Odysseus want that? The question is grammatical, not rhetorical: not "why does he want to kill the suitors?" but "why is the thing that he wants *that*?"

---

54 There is a further technical problem, which becomes important later but must at least be described here: as this is a dream, it represents what she *wishes* Odysseus to want. If she can dream her desire, why not just dream that he desires what *she* wants-- e.g., she dreams that the eagle desires to stay with Calypso? She might know this isn't really his desire, but she can wish it was. Instead, she dreams he wants to return and kill the suitors-- and then wishes she deprives him of his wish. On first pass this seems unnecessarily spiteful-- unless Odysseus's wish to return and kill suitors is not his but *someone else's* wish, and Penelope wishes to deprive *that other person*.

Why Is Odysseus Disguised?

Even the goddess of wiles is baffled (13.370):

> Eagerly would another man on his return from
> wanderings have hastened to behold in his
> halls his children and his wife; but thou art not
> yet minded to know or learn of aught, till thou
> hast furthermore proved thy wife...

Those other eager men hasten home without the benefit
of being told by a god that their wife was after all faithful.
But Athena does tell Odysseus Penelope has been faithful. So
why the delay? And why the disguise of beggar?

It is worth observing that he is almost never called a
beggar. Penelope refers to him as "stranger", while most of
the suitors call him "wanderer" (noun) or "poor" (adjective).
It is Odysseus himself who calls himself a "beggar"
(ἐπιστάτης, suppliant; πτωχός, poor man). There is a very
specific reason for this: it's what he *is*.

It is easy to assume that even Antinous would have been
much more respectful to the wanderer if he had known it was
Odysseus. But what would a *better* man think? What
would-- does-- Odysseus think? If one were to have asked
the outbound Odysseus what his fantasy for the future was, it

would have been the opposite of what happened: Odysseus had put his house on hold and sailed for duty, honor and gain, and returned with nothing-- worse, much worse, *he had lost all of his men.* Odysseus had returned in dishonor.[55]

---

55 Compare Menelaus's return, who was himself delayed 8 years later than Agamemnon, wandering but also profiting (4.75), and returned home bringing more treasure than his ships could even bear (14.310). He generously says he'd give it up if only to have back Agamemnon and all his men who perished in Troy, but such magnanimity is only the privilege of a winner.

Also, Nestor admonishes Telemachus to get home before the suitors devour his wealth and "you will have gone on a fruitless journey"; to be clear based on the history: leaving it to be devoured is worse than what he was doing before, which was being home while it was devoured. What is emphasized is the importance of gaining wealth, giving it to others magnanimously, and protecting it.

This makes the following exchange jarringly unheroic. Odysseus speaks with Alcinous and says:

> Lord Alcinous, renowned above all men, if you
> should bid me abide here even for a year, and should
> further my sending, and give glorious gifts, even
> that would I choose; and it would be better far to
> come with a fuller hand to my dear native land. Aye,
> and I should win more respect and love from all men
> who should see me when I had returned to Ithaca.

In what time, place, or fantasy would receiving gifts for no reason *win* him respect at home? Significantly, Odysseus is indeed *given* treasure-- given honor-- by the Phaeacians guided by Athena, as if he deserved it for who he was. Is this honorable? It is utterly inconceivable that Achilles

81

This is what Odysseus would have thought[56]. Perhaps he still had the physical land, the building, and maybe a woman still inside it; the proper way to return would be humbly, as an ἐπιστάτης, asking the forgiveness of his wife and son for abandoning them for two decades, leaving them to fend for themselves, returning with nothing to compensate them,

---

would accept gifts *as if* it was treasure he won himself, or to make up for losses; but that is exactly Agamemnon's logic that opens the Iliad.

A video game analogy is helpful here. Now that he has been given treasure *for no reason*-- literally for being the main character and for passing through the Phaeacian level-- Athena and Odysseus hide the treasure in a cave. The treasure itself is not necessary any more (Odysseus never refers to it again, and tells Penelope he's just going to rob the suitors-- she must be so proud!); it serves as a needed object to raise his "Honor points", and he moves up a level. Right after he stores the Honor points in his cave, Athena tells him that Penelope makes promises to the suitors but is merely pretending; and Odysseus says, *out loud*, that if he had returned without knowing this, he would have suffered the same fate as Agamemnon (13.380). The key reveal isn't that she is faithful, but that she is lying to the suitors, giving the suitors hope. A wife pretending to be duplicitous is more dangerous than a duplicitous wife, because it leaves open the others' desires.

The treasure gives him "Honor points", which lead to "Information points", and now he's at a high enough level to Return Home. But if Athena had said nothing, what was the risk? Unlike Agamemnon, he wasn't eagerly hastening to go home, clueless and trusting; he was already on alert. Without Athena's information, he would have returned home less trusting of the suitors, more suspicious, even of his wife. That should have been protective. It is inconceivable that he would have been *more likely* to die like Agamemnon if he was suspicious that she was unfaithful. But the video game analogy provides the explanation: without the Honor and the Information points, it would have been impossible in game to *defeat* the suitors, because he would only have been a Level 1 Beggar, not a Level 2 Hero disguised as a beggar.

82

while he-- had sex with Calypso? But to imagine that instead of atoning for the men he lost, he would then kill their kin; that in a feudal patriarchy he would kill two generations of past and future patriarchs; to presume that the goddess of wisdom and war would help him-- no other gods, not even Poseidon, taking the other side of this monomania; to have convinced himself that this would be honorable, celebrated, that it would win him respect and his house-- it is *madness*. It is *magical* thinking[57]. *Odysseus would never have thought*

---

56 Yet, in fact, he does *not* think this, and we should ask why. There is a contrast between the Iliadic versus Odyssean Odysseus that is not sufficiently appreciated but which is central to psychoanalysis. Laertes's greatest moment is when he proudly fights the suitors with his son and grandson. Achilles in Hades derives his only joy in hearing how brave and mighty his son turned out. The Iliadic Odysseus ends up going to Troy precisely because he would not sacrifice his infant son; Menelaus has chronic dysthymia because he has no son; yet the Odyssean Odysseus never cares about what kind of man his *only* son has become, except when he finally needs him to kill his "rivals". He barely even asks about him. Any Greek audience member trying to identify with the story, and any parent, would have been consumed by thoughts of their son. Odysseus may be a husband, but he is not, psychodynamically, a father. There is no Oedipal triangle here for him, neither with his own father nor with his son-- in layman's terms, his struggles are not about his desires in conflict with the "father's" or the "son's"; and this is because they're not his desires, they are Agamemnon's.

57 More correctly: mythological thinking. In psychoanalysis, obsessional thinking is structured as a myth: the obsession takes the prior conflicts of another, and transposes and reorders them, and places them into a mythic structure. It is a psychic repetition of events, most often in his family's history; an unconscious intergenerational transmission. It uses the obsession to transpose unresolved elements in the father's history and resolve them in himself. For example, "marrying your mother" is more often not an Oedipal fantasy about a child's desire, but an obsessional

this.

And no one else thinks it, either. Eupeithes, father of the murdered Antinous, summarizes Odysseus's life's accomplishments:

Friends, a monstrous deed has this man of a

---

attempt at reworking the father's history. It is unconscious; he does not know that marrying her is such an attempt, nor why he feels familiarly unsatisfied in the marriage. The fantasy of Odysseus returning, then besting the suitors; first at a technical skill and then in individual combat; collecting all of their weapons-- it is an acting out of a play, the obsessive's individual myth. The trouble is that it is impossible to bring these two stories-- history and myth-- together; it cannot entirely succeed, one can't settle the dead father's old debts by re-enacting them with a new cast. He will inevitably fail at closing the loop; but by *trying* to make one coincide with the other, he makes a perennially *unsatisfying* turning maneuver, and therefore continues to try. But when this "play" is enacted in an actual play, i.e. not in real life but in an actual story, myth, the loop can be closed by some *author*, some other omnipotent entity; to be clear, it literarily requires *deus ex machina*, for example by a god convincing the suitors' extended families not to descend on the house and retaliate. But this requirement is not a part of the failing of the literary myth as a story; it is the fulfillment of an unconscious wish in an obsessive's individual myth: the myth *causes to exist* some other omnipotent entity.

This may seeming needlessly complicated, elaborate, but it has a quite uncanny precedent. The very phrase *deus ex machina*, "god out of the machine", draws a parallel between the (lazy) literary maneuver that brings extra-narrative power into the story with the literal machine that brought a god into the stage performance. But the parallel is not that a "god" comes in at the end of the story, but that this god was never *in* the story until the end; yet no matter how arbitrary or unsatisfying the god's sudden appearance might seem to be, the fact of the *machine* proves it was already *anticipated* to be necessary. When a movie script is "fixed" to remove *deus ex machina* with a more in-plot consistent solution, the

> truth devised against the Achaeans. Some he
> led forth in his ships, many men and goodly,
> and he has lost his hollow ships, and utterly
> lost his men; and others again has he slain on
> his return...

Odysseus is a blight, a stain on society, he is worse than Trojan. No one thinks he is justified, that he is merely reclaiming his home, that there is honor in what he has done; and if there was any doubt about exactly what kind of a man this Odysseus is perceived to be, Eupeithes then tells the kin they have to hurry because Odysseus may try to *run away*.

> ...verily even in days to come shall we be
> disgraced forever. For a shame is this even for
> men that are yet to be to hear of, if we shall
> not take vengeance on the slayers of our sons
> and our brothers.

Odysseus is irredeemable. But there is one man for whom there was something even more pitiable and dishonorable than the empty handed return of a failed and impoverished general who lost all his men; and that is the

---

movie may be "better" but what is lost is the purpose of the *deus ex machina*, and why so many amateur (or young) writers use it: the story now *causes* god-- some other omnipotent entity-- to exist. Medea already had a legitimate plot solution for her escape over to Athens; so how Medea magically departs is unnecessary and arbitrary, and would never have made the cut if it were a modern movie; yet the *deus ex machina* is there because it is vital to the ancient audience's understanding her story. They *want* Medea to have divine power, because otherwise the person who undid the mighty Jason was just a *wife*.

wealthy return of a victorious general who is then killed, along with all his men, by the wife and rival[58] that had cuckolded him (11.435):

> Ah, verily has Zeus, whose voice is borne afar, visited wondrous hatred on the race of Atreus from the first because of the counsels of women. For Helen's sake many of us perished, and against thee Clytemnestra spread a snare whilst thou wast afar.

It was so shameful a return that his own son had to avenge him, so it was a good thing he had a son, and a good thing the son *literally* wasn't doing anything else and had no other purpose. Can it be said Orestes wanted to? Better to say that he felt compelled to act on Agamemnon's desires and call it the will of the gods. So can we say Odysseus wanted this strange revenge, to kill 108 mostly spoiled dullards for the far lesser sin of-- gluttony? Pride? (Not even lust!) Better to say he felt compelled to act on the same person's desire and call it the will of the gods[59]. Odysseus's plans, part

---

58 It is difficult to say what tradition Homer knew or used; but worth recalling here is the one in which Aegisthus murdered Agamemnon's father, exiled Agamemnon, and then took his wife and ultimately killed him as well.

59 There is a disturbing example of this that should not be dismissed as merely bravado. 9.475, Odysseus has blinded the Cyclops, and is quite pleased with the outcome of his cunning plan-- that he came up with and executed entirely on his own, no gods were involved. He deserves the credit. But instead of claiming it was something he chose to do for his own reasons-- something that is quite true-- he instead *declares* that this was Zeus's-- all the gods'-- punishment of Polyphemus. Only when he is

2 of Penelope's dream, and the rest of the Odyssey are *Agamemnon's* revenge fantasy; and all revenge fantasies are obsessional, driven by envy[60].

It is for this reason that the *question* of Penelope's fidelity must remain open. Odysseus's dead mother (11.165) had told him Penelope was still faithful, seconded by Athena in 13.380, but here Agamemnon weaponizes doubt: probably Penelope is faithful, but when it comes to women, who knows? His advice: return in secret. Reconnaissance-- get to know her again. Do not tell your wife everything; do not be mild with her; do not trust women. Even if you think you know what they want, *you can not know how they will act.*[61]

---

safely out of reach does he take back some credit, mock Polyphemus and reveal his name (all over the protests of his crew). But by doing this, he *makes it true* that he (Odysseus) is the fulfillment of fate, a prophecy for Polyphemus; and who in turn continues the loop by placing Odysseus into his cycle of vengeance, requiring redemption by Poseidon.

60 It is useful to recall Aristotle's distinction between jealousy and envy; jealousy is pain at someone because we want what he has. Envy (φθόνος, phthonos) is pain not because he has what we want, but because he is the one who has it. (Roberts Rhetoric 2004 1387b24-25). φθόνος derives from φθείρω, to defile/corrupt, but it also associates to ὀφθαλμός, eye: it is the seeing that is painful, not the wanting. Aristotle's nuance is highlighted by his use of the word "pain" (lupy); this is more than just the feeling because it carries with it the connotation of its cause, e.g. the difference between "it is a pain" and "it is a harassment" or even "it is a torture." Seeing the other's existence, not lacking the coveted object, is a relentless torture.

61 Even wise Athena (15.20) tells Telemachus to hurry home because if Penelope remarries-- whether she wants the man or not-- his mother may rob him, after all, women who wed again never think of their first husbands, or of their sons, or even of the house. No matter what she

Imprimi Potest

μῆνιν ἄειδε θεὰ Ἀτρεΐδεω Ἀγαμέμνονος

οὐλομένην, ἣ μυρί' Ἀχαιοῖς ἄλγε' ἔθηκε,

πολλὰς δ' ἰφθίμους ψυχὰς Ἄϊδι προΐαψεν

ἡρώων, Διὸς δ' ἐτελείετο βουλή

The final book of the Odyssey opens with Agamemnon in Hades speaking with Achilles. Bygones are bygones, and the two men sing the other's praises: Agamemnon describes Achilles's glorious funeral honors, and Achilles proclaims Agamemnon was Zeus's favorite. But Agamemnon shakes his head. No, he laments, Zeus had instead devised for him a terrible doom.

That he attributes his doom partly or in whole to Zeus is important, we will return to it. Yet before he can tell the tale we readers know so well, he is interrupted by the arrival of the souls of the recently dispatched suitors. He is surprised, he knows these men, they are the "best men". Were they killed in some war?

---

wants, she will try to increase the house of the new man.

88

Amphimedon recounts to Agamemnon how they met their evil end. They had been courting Penelope; Odysseus had come back in disguise; he stole and hid their weapons; he tricked them into the bow contest; and then-- with the help of "some god"-- slaughtered them all, sending their souls to Hades and leaving their bodies to rot.

Such a tale is sure to get a profound response from the emotionally labile King of the Achaeans, complicated perhaps by divided sympathies: both Odysseus and the suitors are men he personally knows, although courting a man's wife is likely to elicit a strong reaction. Either way, Odysseus murdering them is an enormously significant event in the Odyssey, which makes what Agamemnon says about it puzzling: he says absolutely nothing about it. He does not care at all about Odysseus or what he did.

What drives him to euphoria, however, is Penelope and what she didn't do. He declares that the glory of the virtue of Penelope ("daughter of Icarius") will live forever in song-- in contrast to Clytemnestra ("daughter of Tyndareus")[62], who

---

62 Agamemnon, like the dream-eagle, does not refer to Penelope, Helen, or Clytemnestra by their names or as wives of husbands (e.g. "wife of Odysseus"), but as the daughters of their fathers. Their primary identities cannot be as wives, otherwise their actions are about being wives, and what Clytemnestra did becomes her husband's *fault*. In contrast, Clytemnestra is called "wife of Agamemnon" many times by the narration when describing Aegisthus taking and beguiling her (e.g. 1.35), because this explains her crime (against her husband), and also implies some of the fault is Agamemnon's (e.g. for Iphigenia).

One might retort that the phrase "daughter of X" may seem a traditional epithet, but the Odyssey uses it only for goddesses and the unmarried (e.g.

committed an act so vile that it brings "shame on all women, including the women who do good"[63].

Obviously, what makes Penelope so song-worthy is that she… didn't have a suitor stab her husband? Do it herself? It seems a low bar for wifely glory.

Recall the mythology that when the suitors came for Helen to her father Tyndareus's home, he was afraid to get rid of them; it was Odysseus who solved the impasse. Through

---

Eurycleia, Nausicaa); the only married women referred to as "daughter of" are the questionable wives Clytemnestra and Penelope. Compare the labels of the other famous Achaean women: e.g. Tyro "daughter of Salmoneus and *said to be* wife of Cretheus" (11.235); Antiope (unmarried) "daughter of Asopus"; Alcmene "wife of Amphitryon" (11.265). Interestingly, Helen is also not referred to as wife of her husband, but neither is she referred to as anyone's daughter (Lede is safely "the wife of Tyndareus", however (11.295)), except two instances which border on irony: 22.225, Athena reminds Odysseus of 9 years he spent fighting for "high-born" Helen; and the narration describes the "daughter of Zeus" secretly giving a "forgetting" drug (received from the "wife of Thon") to Menelaus and the others so that she can (safely) tell the tale of "forsaking my child, my bridal chamber, and my husband".

63 He does not mention the shame brought by the other daughter of Tyndareus, Helen. This is psychologically important: We all know why Clytemnestra was worse, but we are not told why she is worse. The Odyssey never refers to her motivation, or that Clytemnestra even *contributed* to Agamemnon's death. The Odyssey does explicitly remark that Helen tried to contribute directly to her husband's murder by trying to lure them out of the Trojan Horse. The fantasy of what she did becomes limited by information. But just as Agamemnon's murder occurs "off stage", i.e outside of the Iliad and Odyssey, and the audience is left to imagine-- project-- a personalized version of the events, so too is the audience allowed to project the motivations and actions of Clytemnestra-- and why they were so much worse.

his negotiations, Helen was betrothed to Menelaus (in absentia). Penelope's betrothal was part of the same back room deal between Icarius, Tyndareus, and Odysseus; but unlike Helen, she was given the power (by her father) to choose whether or not she wanted Odysseus. Importantly, what she has to do to signal she wants Odysseus is to *not to act*-- not look back, passively be lead by an other to what she wants.

The story of Helen's abduction by Theseus and Paris is well known; to what extent she desired to go with any of these men (or even back with Menelaus) is not. But as an "abduction", she semantically, *logically*, could not have chosen it, no matter what she desired. Agamemnon cares nothing about her desires; that she does not *choose* is the crucial fact. Penelope (23.215) gives an interesting commentary:

> So he spoke, and her knees were loosened where she sat, and her heart melted, as she knew the sure tokens which Odysseus told her. Then with a burst of tears she ran straight toward him, and flung her arms about the neck of Odysseus, and kissed his head... "But be not now wroth with me for this, nor full of indignation, because at the first, when I saw thee, I did not thus give thee welcome. For always the heart in my breast was full of dread, lest some man should come and beguile me with his words; for there are many that plan devices of evil."

91

"Knees loosened" likely darkens that first sentence; but even without this, there is something amiss about the relationship between her fearing being "beguiled" and not recognizing Odysseus. The easy answer is she simply closed herself off to all men so as not to be... seduced? Was she afraid she could be seduced?

To clarify this, in the very next sentence, she uses Helen and Paris as an example. The analogy might seem predictable-- except that the official story is Helen was abducted. Was she also seduced?

> Nay, even Argive Helen, daughter of Zeus, would not have lain in love with a man of another folk had she known that the warlike sons of the Achaeans were to bring her home again.

Apparently *neither*: the beguiling was convincing Helen that the Achaeans wouldn't come after her. She neither chose to be faithful (and was thus abducted against her will) nor did she choose to cheat on her husband with Paris. Penelope suggests Helen perhaps even wanted Paris, but she chose nothing. This is the analogy Penelope is inadvertently making: Penelope closed herself off to all men so that she would not choose either fidelity or a new man. To reinforce this, her next sentence is that Helen didn't choose to cheat; a god "caused" her to do it. Helen wasn't cheating on Menelaus-- i.e. thinking she'd then return to him-- she says she thought she was being taken away, forever. Helen didn't choose to stay or go-- she doesn't choose any relationship;

she gets put into them[64]. It is a subtle distinction, but matters to Agamemnon because it is about who has the power to choose. When women choose things-- even good things-- bad things happen. Following from this, none of the three central women "cheated" on their husbands; Penelope did not have sex and the other two were leaving their husbands. But

---

64 i.e. that the choice Helen was making was not whether to cheat, but whether to stop the cheating that was already in progress. It is a materially meaningless distinction that is of great psychic significance. The difficulty is translating the sentence "she would not have lain with Paris *had* she known they would come", given that is written in the indicative. The inferences in such a conditional are best captured with the subjunctive, and modal logic, but Penelope repeatedly uses propositional logic (indicative) as a way of *causing* something to be true. In this case, the conditional can be written as:

"she would not have cheated if she had known"

NOT CHEATED if KNOWN <=>

If KNOWN then NOT CHEATED

Penelope's unconscious is rigorously logical, and we can work through the implications:

1) If she had KNOWN, then NOT CHEATED. (p then ~q)

NOT CHEATED does not imply KNOWN (~q then p; converse, false)

NOT KNOWN does not imply CHEATED (~p therefore ~~q, false, fallacy of denying the antecedent)

CHEATED does imply NOT KNOWN (~~q therefore ~p, modus tollens)

Clytemnestra is terrifyingly unique because she chose to have sex with Aegisthus. And chose to murder. She acted. The vile act that she committed that brings shame to women-- even good women who *do* good-- was not infidelity but specifically acting on her own desires.

Helen is the danger of feminine sexuality without will

The key question is how to understand the interaction between the CHEATING and the KNOWING. According to the logic, KNOWING they would come is *a sufficient* condition for her NOT CHEATING. But can it be correct that NOT CHEATING is *the necessary* condition for her to KNOW they would come-- as if cheating would retroactively change the truth of her knowledge?

There is a way this could work: if it is not Helen who decides what is true. A legal example is helpful: a person steals $50k from another man. He lies in court, saying this was a voluntary payment for some service he claims he performed. His lie is believed, and he is acquitted. Nevertheless, he is soon charged with tax evasion since it has *become* true that he earned the money. For Penelope, here as a proxy for Agamemnon, Helen doesn't have the power to act; if she knows he'll come for her, she won't cheat; but also, *in order* for her to know he would come for her, it is necessary that she could never have cheated. If she did cheat—if she is ever caught in flagrante delicto, then it must have been true that she NEVER KNEW. This is a very common atemporal logic that, in modern times, is mostly seen in the reverse: if you constantly accuse your wife of cheating, she'll cheat, proving she was a cheater. But there is an important historical parallel: in the 5th century Athens, if an adulteress was caught "in the act"-- ἐπ' αὐτοφώρῳ-- normal judicial process could be bypassed and judgment decided by the magistrates (e.g. Lysias 13.85, Antiphon 1.3). But whatever the rule meant, the implementation of this rule made it clear that no actual observer needed to catch her; "caught in the act" was applied retroactively, to explain the appropriateness of summary judgment by the magistrates. In simple terms, if the magistrates were hearing the case, then she must have been caught in the act, and her guilt self-evident. Note the literal translation of αὐτοφώρῳ is "self-

94

that is passive to the desires of others, and ends up married to one man, abducted by two, and dragged back by thousands. Her twin Clytemnestra is her antithesis, she represents too much desire and too much will, masculine will: she chose Aegisthus, chose to have Agamemnon be murdered (or murder him herself)-- and even chose to pursue vengeance on her son. *Neither "daughter of Tyndareus" wants what her husband wants; and Clytemnestra dares to act on her desires.*

---

detected", reinforcing the idea that the application of the term is sufficient to cause it to be true even for oneself. Interestingly, the use of this phrase disappears with Athens, only to resurface in a single but prominent textual instance 400 (or 1400) years later: John 8:4, the mob asks Jesus if they should stone an adulteress that was caught in the act, κατείληπται ἐπ' αὐτοφώρῳ. Tellingly, neither the husband nor the lover are present. Necessarily, neither are the Romans.

Although not applicable here, it is interesting to contrast this with explanation given by Euripides's Helen for why she ran off with Paris. She gives a long passage blaming it on the heart, on the passions (notably analyzed by Gorgias) only to finally blurt out the truth: it was Menelaus's fault, he shouldn't have left her alone with him, *what did he expect would happen*? Helen's answer is the kind of subversion characteristic of Euripides, and recall the adultery laws had been changed only recently by Pericles to *include* a legal punishment for the adulterous wife where before there was none-- i.e. now legally implying that a woman *could* choose. Homeric Helen did not ask the question the 5th century Athenians had to consider: is it better if I am mindless property you were too stupid to guard, or that I chose someone over you? Her Euripidean response to Menelaus also challenged the Greeks on how to understand the meaning of beauty: did Helen's beauty make her more desirable and more likely for him to act, or did her beauty make her more desirous-- and therefore more likely for her to act? One should not too hastily answer through modern conceptualizations of power imbalances without carefully considering the Athenians' contemporary real life ambivalence about desire, desirability, and demagoguery-- about Alcibiades.

This is, of course, the father's fault, not the husbands'. Penelope is Agamemnon's ideal, the feminine synthesis of both: still present is Helen's desirability but not her passivity. Like Clytemnestra she has her own desires, but not her will to act. Penelope is desirable, she has desire; yet she will not act: she gets what she wants by not acting, and (as far as Agamemnon can tell) she wants what her husband wants.

Agamemnon's canonization of Penelope is not for her fidelity, which even Menelaus would hardly consider miraculous. In fact, Agamemnon does not have any idea whether she has been faithful (he didn't even know Odysseus had returned or killed anyone). All Agamemnon knows of her subplot is what Amphimedon tells him in Hades, which is limited:

1. she neither refused a hateful marriage, nor brought it to pass

2. she contrived their death and a black doom

3. she told the wooers to be patient until she finished the shroud

4. by day she weave at the loom, by night she unraveled it, for three years

5. by her cunning she kept it from their notice

6. she finally finished it, not because she wanted to, but because she was compelled

7. she washed it and showed it to them, it shined like the sun, and [then] the god sent Odysseus back

8. by command of Odysseus, she set out the bow for the contest.

Observe that #8 is factually false-- the bow contest was her idea, she herself had already decided to do this-- but Agamemnon does not know that, he is told that Odysseus *commanded* her to do it. Thus, what Agamemnon praises is only what he knows. Take special note of #1: Agamemnon does not condemn her passivity, he praises it. Nowhere does he applaud her for her desires, because he does not care about those. Certainly, she appeared to want what (Agamemnon thinks) her husband wanted-- which is what Agamemnon wants. But no matter what she might have desired, her proper place is not to act. Penelope maintained the status quo. But we must be very precise: the status quo Agamemnon praises her for maintaining is *post* bellum, it *contains* the suitors[65].

---

65 It would be a sufficient parallel that Agamemnon "kills" Clytemnestra's suitor through Odysseus's killing of Penelope's suitors. But the text sets up a much more complex, satisfying, revenge. Fagles's translation of Penelope's dream:

> The geese were your <u>suitors</u> — I was once the eagle
> but now I am your husband, back again at last,
> **about to launch a terrible fate against them all!**

The Greek of Penelope's dream has a slightly different emphasis:

> ὃς πᾶσι <u>μνηστῆρσιν</u> ἀεικέα πότμον ἐφήσω

> on all the <u>wooers</u> I will bring down a *shameful destiny.*

97

What she did that was praiseworthy is *not* getting rid of them-- sex or no-- she maintained the rival(s) until her husband returned so that he could have the honor and satisfaction of killing them.

This is what Agamemnon praises. Her fidelity is incidental. Her desire is irrelevant. *She does not act[66].*

The crucial transition in the Odyssey from a story about Odysseus's desire to the one about Agamemnon's obsessive desire occurs at their meeting in Hades. Agamemnon causes Odysseus to *want* to return home the way Agamemnon with hindsight wishes he had returned: a hero, *disguised* as a beggar, doing reconnaissance; then destroying the guilty rival; and while leaving the wife alive, he and his noble and only son destroy all of the possibilities of a wife's personal desires; obliterating her will and ensuring her role as passive wife of

---

The eagle/Odysseus/Agamemnon wants to understand the killing not just as vengeance, but as part of shameful destiny. Upon whom? The word wooers, μνηστῆρας, is repeated twice, and has special association to Agamemnon's wife, Κλυταιμνήστρη, Clytemnestra (compare Aeschylus's Clytemestra Κλυταιμήστρα.) Killing the wooers counts towards the killing of his "well wooed" wife.

66 It can not be overemphasized how important this Homeric *idea* of proper women being inactive (which will be used as a defense against men's impotence) will be to *later* Greek society. Literary examples abound, but consider Pericles's Funeral oration's penultimate paragraph, in which he tells the women that their proper role is mourning, or silent. This cannot be an example of the pervasiveness of patriarchal power but rather evidence of its dissipation, because in order for Pericles to have felt it necessary to say this out loud, then it must have been increasingly not true.

husband[67].

The story would have been very different without that meeting. Penelope might have dreamt of a continuation of the status quo, under the guise she wants her husband to return. If the shroud had been finished, Odysseus would have returned but in dishonor, not disguised as a beggar but having become a beggar; and 108 noblemen courting his former wife would have been shocked not that he had managed to return but that he had dared to return. He would have been turned away or attacked; he would have left, or fought. Had he fought and killed any of the suitors, there would have been justifiable retaliation by the suitors' families-- who does this beggar think he is?   His privilege as noble hero and lord of the house had been revoked. He would have won, or lost; there would have been more fighting, or a truce under conditions. The Odyssey would have been more like the Iliad: historical fiction, not mythology.

But the Odyssey stands as Agamemnon's dream. Caught within this dream is Odysseus, and crushed under both of them is Penelope. This is why Penelope dreams her dream within a dream in Book 19 when the Odyssey is almost over, and not in Book I, where, supporting the conventional

---

67 Orestes kills Clytemnestra in the Oresteia, but in the Odyssey it only explicitly says he killed Aegisthus.   This is again interpretable as Agamemnon's wish: there was at least *a* logic to Aegisthus's actions, and fit a mythico-historical context, so his death is the proper revenge. There is no logic to what Clytemnestra did (she should not have *done* anything) so her death is not satisfying to him, the proper revenge would be to deprive her of her desires, take away her will-- neuter her, and turn her (back) into a wife.

interpretation, it could serve as background for her story. It is the end of her story, her corner of a magic-- mythic-- square in which the total in every direction must be the same: from what she wants to what Odysseus wants her to want, which is what Agamemnon wanted him to want her to want, all because Clytemnestra wanted and acted on her own.

In Penelope's own dreams her latent wish manifests, and it is for the destruction of Odysseus's desires-- of Agamemnon's desires. But not only can she not act on these desires, she cannot even have them even in her dreams, they are taken from her, as the eagle, Odysseus, Agamemnon and we omnipotently declare her wish to be their opposite. Penelope does not get to have a story of her own. She is a tool for the satisfaction of others. The most she can do for breathing room is keep the loop open, maintain the status quo.

Freud never attempted an interpretation of Penelope's famous dream from the Odyssey. He did, however, begin his *Interpretation Of Dreams* with a famous quote from the Aeneid, which begins a passage that ironically *is literally* the interpretation of Penelope's dream. If only Freud had taken his own advice and listened to the words:

> If I cannot bend the higher powers, I will move hell. To bar him from his throne exceeds my fated power. So be it!... But long delays I still can plot, and to the high event deferment and obstruction. I can smite the subjects of both kings. Let sire and son buy with their people's blood this marriage bond...

100

Plot and obstruct, defer and delay. If you don't have the power to pursue your desires, you can at least deprive the other of theirs. Who knows-- maintain the status quo long enough and some omnipotent entity might abruptly end the story, apply a forgetting spell, and wake the dreamer up.

Aporia

What Is The Purpose Of The Odyssey?

We can conclude with a general psychoanalytic thesis for which only a brief summary can be given here.

The ancient Greeks, especially the 7th and 6th century Greeks who solidified Homeric songs into comparatively stable poetry, had every reason to celebrate the Iliad. But not the Odyssey. There were no heroes in the Odyssey; it was a spin-off based on a secondary character of dubious merit who accomplished a dishonorable goal not through bravery and might but because a god inexplicably sided with him. To whom was this story worth telling?   What we know of the Cyclops can be told to boys; but the empty handed return of a man who lost all his men is hardly worth asking the Muse to tell us about.

But the Odyssey could have utility as a myth, not to romanticize Man's longing to Return Home but to sublimate the anxiety of what a man might find back at the house. You took your life in your hands when you left for adventure, but your life was in someone else's when you tried to return, and recall that Oedipus was warned not to go home, Theseus was told how to go home, and Nicias was afraid to even try. He was right.

Every civilization has a founding history that becomes increasingly mythologized with the passage of time; but the Greeks were peculiar in that the Peisistratid myth was demonstrably false, there were people still alive who had lived through the events themselves. Yet they could not publicly accept the factual story of their own origin, urgently disavowing a truth that was evidently inscribed in stone, because rather than the story of democratic revolution won with honor and bravery it involved a pointless murder driven by lust and envy, not to mention requiring salvation by the Spartans. They had to rewrite history in their mind, exalt the crime, apotheosize the murderers and switch the bodies; wipe down the scene with bleach and then build powerful new statues to declare it true. The culture that was becoming omnipotent had to fool itself.

Neither could Agamemnon's story be told as objective history, it was the all too real manifestation of the anxiety of a culture whose greatest threats were not foreign but quite literally domestic. What can one do with the story of a mighty king who set out and conquered, who survived 10 years of war and needed no god to assist him, who returned in triumph and on schedule bearing the honor and spoils of war-- only to be killed by nothing more than his wife and rival? For no reason? For no *purpose?* It wasn't that such a thing was impossible, but that it was unthinkable; even Medea had deus ex machina, not to escape but to cause to be true that the preceding events were not done by an ordinary wife. How could Agamemnon's life and death make sense

103

after such pettiness? Defeated by-- a woman? Who would redeem him? A new kind of hero was needed, someone with particular abilities suited to the purpose, not bravery and strength but deception and cunning. A man with the wiles of-- a woman.

The history is thus transformed into myth, the impossible redemption of the best man is accomplished through the impossible redemption of No Man by harmonizing the two simultaneously.   Dishonored Odysseus is consciously redeemed by acting out the unconscious redemption of honored Agamemnon: the form of the story that can be told solves the problem of the story that cannot be thought. It is the manifestation of a wish, in its distorted form. Now both stories have necessity and purpose, causing them to be destined by the omnipotent gods who open and close such epic cycles. The gods have declared it to be true: it was for Agamemnon that Odysseus left for Kakoilion, and it is for him he must return.

Sing to us, oh Muse, of *that*.

No matter how effective unconscious defenses are at maintaining the psychic status quo, they are often impotent against the contingencies of real world. The next defense is to retreat into omniscience: "learning how things really work", "knowing who really has power", why and "for what purpose". Sadly, pornographization has always been the result: the reduction of fantasy into the concrete, under the guise that it is more detailed; the repression of fantasy, returning as information. First Agamemnon's story was only told obliquely, in other people's stories, leaving the hearer to imagine the details. By the 5th century some fantasies could finally be thought *out loud*, men were able to explicitly watch Clytemnestra herself as the direct actor of the murder, and the revenge and redemption cycle that it necessitated. But this was not because the Golden Age Greeks had substantially increased psychic maturity, but because the ambiguities of the previous fantasies had become intolerable. They did not yet need to watch a graphic depiction of his wife murdering him in his own kingdom, or watch a woman even pretend to have that kind of power, it was then sufficient to have a male Clytemnestra appear on stage and describe it, out loud. Now the fantasy had become something real enough, and to make sure it was real enough for the Athenians demos, Agamemnon's kingdom was moved out of Sparta.

Every repressed thought reflexively leaves a residue of its repression, this is the lingering odor of bleach in an uncannily empty room; this is the return of the repressed. The success of a psychic defense depends on whether the bleach worked; whether some other omnipotent entity notices the bleach; and, if he does, whether he can be fooled into declaring it means something else.

But what if he can't be fooled? If we want our god to be not the solution to our problems, but the cause-- so that it can't be our fault-- what would such a god think about our *trying* to fool him? What did the Greeks think he would think?

The well known opening line of the Odyssey is the poet's

request for the Muse to sing about a certain man: ἄνδρα μοι ἔννεπε, μοῦσα, πολύτροπον…

Of course it will be the poet who sings, the Muse will inspire him, sing through him, sing through the poet's unconscious the story of Odysseus.

It is significant, therefore, that the unconscious decides to begin the story not with Odysseus but with Zeus, and not because Zeus has anything to do with Odysseus, but because he has nothing to do with him. Zeus is omnipotent and also omniscient, yet it opens with him not knowing; he is troubled, confused, shaken, not by the story of Odysseus but by the significance of the story of someone ostensibly unrelated: Aegisthus.

This is what occupies the king of the gods, and modern readers might be forgiven for only having a vague recollection of what he said or that he had said anything; even Athena dismissively derails his short speech and impatiently demands to know why Zeus has brought such a terrible fate on Odysseus, and what he is going to do next.

Those ironic words that escape her mouth only increase Zeus's bewilderment. The patron goddess of Western Civilization was offered a glimpse of omniscience, and instead demanded from him omnipotence. As above, so below.

Who today gives any thought to Zeus's sobering monologue-- the very argument of the Odyssey? Yet full of pride we will recite the epic's opening invocation to the Muse as if it proved our initiation into its mysteries. But salvation comes not by being seduced by the sound of a siren's song we still can't agree how to sing but by listening to the words of those who know, for there is wisdom; they reveal the anxieties of the ancient Greeks and are a rebuke to the defenses of our modern age, they are the first words said *out loud* in the Odyssey and come directly from the mouth of their god, he who has ears to hear let him hear:

> ὢ πόποι, οἷον δή νυ θεοὺς βροτοὶ αἰτιόωνται·
> ἐξ ἡμέων γάρ φασι κάκ᾽ ἔμμεναι, οἱ δὲ καὶ
> αὐτοὶ σφῇσιν ἀτασθαλίῃσιν ὑπὲρ μόρον ἄλγε᾽
> ἔχουσιν

> *Look now*, how ready mortals are to blame the gods. It is from us, they say, that evils come, but they even of themselves, through their own blind folly, have sorrows beyond that which is ordained.

Watch what you hear. I have safely used the Murray translation, where he has generously declared that ὢ πόποι is to mean *Look now*, but sadly, it cannot, let this loosen your knees and melt your heart: the first words spoken out loud in the Odyssey are not words but the sound of a word, the naming of a word, an onomatopoeia; it is the sound of exasperation, the sound of disbelief, the sound of a god who despite his omniscience has no words for what he sees in the human psyche. Watch what you hear: it is the sound of a god spitting in disgust.

107

Printed in Great Britain
by Amazon